Visions of a Better World

A UNITED NATIONS PEACE MESSENGER PUBLICATION

EDITED BY
THE BRAHMA KUMARIS WORLD SPIRITUAL UNIVERSITY

Global Cooperation for a Better World
a Peace Messenger Initiative dedicated
to the United Nations presents

VISIONS

OF A

EDITORIAL COMMITTEE
Jagdish Chander Hassija
Mohini Panjabi

COMPILATION AND WRITING
Christopher Drake
Nicholaa Malet de Carteret
Gayatri Naraine

CONSULTANTS
Helen Churko Lord Ennals
James Jonah Robin Ludwig
Steve Naraine Christian Rolling

BETTER
WORLD

**GLOBAL CO-OPERATION
FOR A BETTER WORLD**

Peace Messenger Initiative
dedicated to the
United Nations

VISIONS OF A BETTER WORLD

A United Nations Peace Messenger Publication

Published by
Brahma Kumaris World Spiritual University (UK)
Global Cooperation House
65 Pound Lane
London NW10 2HH, UK
ISBN 0-9637396-8-9 (Soft Cover)
ISBN 0-9637396-9-7 (Hard Cover)

First Edition 1993
Reprinted, with minor amendments, 1994

Designed by Ananta Printing and Publishing, Soquel, California, USA
Printed through Palace Press International, San Francisco, USA by Kwong Fat Offset Printing, Hong Kong
For every tree used in producing paper for this book, the printers have ensured that two more trees have been planted.

Compiled and edited by the Brahma Kumaris World Spiritual University (BKWSU), a non-governmental organization
affiliated to the United Nations Department of Public Information; in consultative status with the United Nations
Economic and Social Council, and UNICEF; a Peace Messenger Organization and the coordinators of the Global
Cooperation for a Better World project, a Peace Messenger Initiative dedicated to the United Nations. The views and
opinions contained herein and attributed to specified person(s) are those of the person(s) so specified. Such views or
opinions do not necessarily reflect the view or position of the BKWSU, the United Nations or any other person(s)
elsewhere herein mentioned.

This United Nations Peace Messenger Publication is being published for educational purposes. The BKWSU is a
non-profit organization and all royalties and sale proceeds are applied to help further its charitable activities and to
facilitate subsidized distribution of this and other publications.

Cover Visuals: Front cover: "World Peace", William Sawicki, USA
Back cover: "Once there was a planet", Brian Young, Japan
Children of Kilburn Park School, London, Eugene Romain, UK

ACKNOWLEDGEMENTS

The Brahma Kumaris are extremely grateful to countless individuals, organizations and businesses around the world for their cooperation, assistance and advice in the implementation of the Global Cooperation project and the preparation of this book. Many, many thanks to the project's international and national advisory committee members, patrons, sponsors and other helpers in all the countries involved; without you it would have been no more than a dream.....

GLOBAL COOPERATION FOR A BETTER WORLD
INTERNATIONAL ADVISORY COMMITTEE

PRESIDENT:
Dadi Prakashmani (Head of the Brahma Kumaris)

HONORARY CHAIR:
Mrs. Marcela Perez de Cuellar

CO-CHAIRS:
Dr. James O. C. Jonah (Under-Secretary-General of the United Nations)
Lord Ennals (Member, British House of Lords)

MEMBERS:
H. R. H. Princess Basma Bint Talal, Jordan
Genrich Borovik, Russia
Jacques-Yves Cousteau, France
The Rt. Hon. Malcolm Fraser, C.H., Australia
Ms. Helena Kekkonen, Finland
Miss Margaret Wambui Kenyatta, Kenya
Sir Laurence Muir, Australia
Dr. Robert Muller, France
Krzysztof Ostrowski, Poland
Senator Leticia Ramos Shahani, Philippines
H. E. Madame Tien Soeharto, Indonesia
Jeana Yeager, USA
UN Coordinator: Dr. Robin Ludwig

INTERNATIONAL COORDINATORS:
Brian Bacon
Michael George
Jayanti Kirpalani
Nicholaa Malet de Carteret
Mohini Panjabi

LEADERS OF VISION

The Rt. Hon. Malcolm Fraser, C.H., *Australia*   page 166
Mark Eyskens, *Belgium*   *p. 166*
Leo Tindemans, *Belgium*   *p. 166*
President Q.K.J. Masire, *Botswana*   *p. 166*
Brian Mulroney, *Canada*   *p. 166*
President Patricio Aylwin, *Chile*   *p. 167*
Oscar Arias Sanchez, *Costa Rica*   *p. 167*
President Sir Clarence Seignoret, *Commonwealth of Dominica*   *p. 168*
Hugh Desmond Hoyte, *Guyana*   *p. 169*
Steingrimur Hermannsson, *Iceland*   *p. 169*
Rajiv Gandhi, *India*   *p. 169*
Madame Tien Soeharto, *Indonesia*   *p. 73*
Chaim Herzog, *Israel*   *p. 169*
Ephraim Katzir, *Israel*   *p. 170*
H.R.H. Princess Basma Bint Talal, *Jordan*   *p. 170*
Prime Minister Dr. Mahathir bin Mohamad, *Malaysia*   *p. 172*
Dr. Siti Hasmah Bte Haji Mohd Ali, *Malaysia*   *p. 152*
President Censu Tabone, *Malta*   *p. 172*
Prime Minister Sir Anerood Jugnauth, *Mauritius*   *p. 172*
Lady Jugnauth, *Mauritius*   *p. 72*
President Sam Nujoma, *Namibia*   *p. 172*
The Rt. Hon. Nagendra Prasad Rijal, *Nepal*   *p. 173*
Governor-General Dame Catherine Tizard, *New Zealand*   *p. 173*
Russell Marshall, *New Zealand*   *p. 173*
President Violeta B. de Chamorro, *Nicaragua*   *p. 173*
Prime Minister Mrs. Gro Harlem Brundtland, *Norway*   *p. 174*
Corazon Aquino, *Philippines*   *p. 18*
President Lech Walesa, *Poland*   *p.175*
Mikhail S. Gorbachev, *Russia*   *p. 175*
Prime Minister Felipe Gonzalez Marquez, *Spain*   *p.176*
Turgut Ozal, *Turkey*   *p.176*
Vice-President Samson B.M. Kisekka, *Uganda*   *p.176*
Prime Minister John Major, *United Kingdom*   *p.177*
George Bush, *United States of America*   *p.177*
Jimmy Carter, *United States of America*   *p.178*
Abdul Aziz Abdul Ghani, *Yemen*   *p.178*

VOICES

Mohammed Ali   *p. 34*
Cardinal Paulo Evaristo Arns   *p. 105*
Vladimir Ashkenazy   *p. 88*
Lloyd Bridges   *p. 102*
James Burke   *p. 116*
Montserrat Caballe   *p. 33*
Helen Caldicott   *p. 52*
Celia Cruz   *p. 89*
Ariel Dorfman   *p. 42*
William H. Draper III   *p. 185*
Yves Duteil   *p. 79*
Emmanuel   *p. 48*
Lord Ennals   *p. 124*
Rabbi Schlomo Goren   *p. 81*
James Grant   *p. 182*
Susan Hampshire   *p. 71*
Peter Hansen   *p. 184*
Sir Edmund Hillary   *p. 84*
Srichand P. Hinduja   *p. 75*
Barbara Marx Hubbard   *p. 16*
V.R. Krishna Iyer   *p. 96*
James Jonah   *p. 4*
Petra Kelly   *p. 24*
Sir William Keys   *p. 96*
Thomas Kleininger   *p. 81*
Fela Anikulapo-Kuti   *p. 104*
H.H. The Dalai Lama   *p. 10*
Richard Leakey   *p. 135*
Jack Lemmon   *p. 60*

Dennis Lillee   *p. 29*
Jan Martenson   *p. 183*
Robert McNamara   *p. 93*
Lord Menuhin   *p. 147*
Edgar Mitchell   *p. 113*
Robert Muller   *p. 33*
Hiroshi Nakajima   *p. 182*
Olivia Newton John   *p. 55*
Gloria Nikoi   *p. 41*
Gabriel Okara   *p. 83*
Javier Perez de Cuellar   *p. 180*
Jonathon Porritt   *p. 52*
Sir Shridath Ramphal   *p.185*
The Rt. Rev. Robert Runcie   *p. 85*
Nafis Sadik   *p. 181*
Ramanand Sagar   *p. 81*
Lea Salonga   *p. 24*
John Sculley   *p. 98*
Leticia Shahani   *p. 188*
Cardinal Sin   *p. 41*
Sir Garfield Sobers   *p. 38*
Chamlong Srimuang   *p. 33*
Maurice Strong   *p. 184*
Mostafa Tolba   *p. 184*
Archbishop Desmond Tutu   *p. 83*
Jon Wynne-Tyson   *p. 50*
Dennis Weaver   *p. 24*
Sally Yeh   *p. 61*
Michael York   *back cover*

CONTENTS

Preface   DADI PRAKASHMANI xi

Foreword   SIR PETER USTINOV xii

Chapter 1   A MILLION MINUTES OF PEACE 1

Chapter 2   HOW TO USE THIS BOOK 7

Chapter 3   THE VALUE OF THE SELF 19

Chapter 4   THE GLOBAL VISION 27

THE GLOBAL VISION STATEMENT 28
   1.   The Joy of Life 30
   2.   Human Rights, Dignity and Integrity 36
   3.   In Balance with Nature 44
   4.   Needs Basic to Life 54
   5.   Educating Mind and Spirit 62
   6.   Family: The World's Warm Core 70
   7.   Respect, Understanding and Tolerance 78
   8.   Communicating with Goodwill 86
   9.   Justice and Law 92
 10.   Democratic Government and People Participation 100
 11.   Science and the Quality of Life 110
 12.   Freedom and Responsibility 118

Chapter 5   A VISION AND A TASK CAN CHANGE THE WORLD..........123
   1.   Plans and Actions 127
   2.   Principles of Cooperation 146

Chapter 6   THE VISIONS OF LEADERS 165

Chapter 7   INTERNATIONAL REFLECTIONS 179

Chapter 8   WE THE PEOPLES FOR A BETTER WORLD..........................187

APPENDICES

I   What is your Vision of a Better World? 192

II   On Running Creative Groups and Roundtables..193

III   The Global Vision Seminar 197

IV   Cooperation in the Classroom 199

V   United Nations Peace Messengers 202

VI   Participating Countries 203

VII A Note on the Editors..205

Beatrix M. Stampfli, Switzerland

United Nations Secretary-General, H.E. Boutros Boutros-Ghali receiving a copy of VISIONS OF A BETTER WORLD from Lord Ennals, Co-chair of Global Cooperation for a Better World International Advisory Committee, following a meeting of the Advisory Group for the 50th Anniversary of the United Nations in Geneva.

Dadi Prakashmani

PREFACE

This book focuses entirely on hopeful visions of the future. It ignores the negative. This is deliberate. As the world nears the end of Kali Yuga, or the dark age, the negative forces in the world will intensify. To counter that, to help bring about the predominance of good when the time comes for the epochal transition out of this grim period, we must concentrate as never before on the positive.

The global conversion from negative to positive energy must be rooted in a heightening of individual consciousness, of a world-wide awakening of the human spirit. We believe that when individuals become aware of their true nature, their innate and unique worth, they cannot be evil. For the spiritually aware person is in touch with the great and universal force for good that we call God.

The testimony of people from around the world, collected in the following pages, makes clear that the process of transformation from evil to good is under way. It is our hope that this book will help intensify and broaden it.

B. K. Prakash Mani.

Dadi Prakashmani
Brahma Kumaris World Spiritual University
Mt. Abu, India

FOREWORD

Sir Peter Ustinov
(UNICEF/Horst Cerni)

The individual is intrinsically more important than the masses, and the currency in the discussion of spiritual values must always be the individual as opposed to the mass, which is composed of nothing but individuals who have temporarily lost their identities in the unfeeling heart of a collectivity.

If proof were needed of this sweeping allegation, consider the fact that no idea has ever arisen out of a collectivity. True, a forum or committee, a parliament, or even, at a pinch, a cabinet, may improve an idea, make it workable or viable. By the same token, they can ruin an idea, distort it, misunderstand it, override it, quash it; but they can never have it in the first place. Ideas are born in the minds of human beings just as children are conceived in the human womb. Not without reason is an idea sometimes called a brain child.

Democracy, along with every major religion, is based very much on the primordial nature of the individual, attempting to guarantee the rights of the individual within the collectivity in one case, and preaching the sacred nature of the immortal soul in the other. The Greeks, to their eternal credit, did substantially more than give democracy its name; they practised it before finding a name for it. For a highly volatile, yet reflective and philosophically inclined people, faced with a forest of question marks, their formulation of democracy was a gigantic step in creating the necessary accommodation between the solitary person and the surrounding society.

Democracy sets rules within the imperfections of a ceaselessly shifting community, and attempts to make sure, by its safeguards and rituals, that the smallest voice will be heard, for who can tell if the smallest voice does not express the best ideas?

Certainly, in a sense, democracy depends for its effect on the very instability inherent in human affairs. After all, if all thought were constant, and nobody ever changed their mind, there would be no point to democracy. It would become as static, and as stagnant, as dictatorship.

Of course, democracy is merely a structure for the control of societies by themselves. It is not a plan of any kind, since it admits of contradictions, of debate, of consensus. The more rampant social theories admit of no contradictions. That is their tactical strength and their strategic weakness. It is never easy to be pragmatic with a blueprint once things go wrong, and contrary conditions make quick changes in rigid designs urgently necessary. Democracy is permanently pragmatic, making provision for every caprice of the climate, for every pull of the current or change in the wind.

Not unnaturally, there is an intellectual desire for something more satisfying than a mere structure. Man has an inherent need to believe in something, and it is in response to this need that social theories as well as religions have sprouted in their bewildering profusion. The world would be far poorer without this permanent cauldron of ideas. It would also be far less dangerous. The problem, therefore, is to preserve and even encourage the human proclivity for divisive beliefs while taking the sting out of the possible consequences of disagreement.

Ideally, men should be judged by their actions not by their beliefs. This is still sadly far from being the case. Whereas religions have succeeded in elevating mankind to wonderful isolated examples of spiritual strength, their message of love, concord, or even tolerance has been tragically ignored by those who use faith as something by its very nature divisive, exclusive and true to the detriment of other truths.

And yet, despite these threats to the world's peace of mind, enormous changes in our sense of values are thrillingly discernible.

At long last, there seems to be a growing realization that interdependence is the best guarantee of independence. There have been attempts in some quarters to give the word federalism a pejorative connotation, and curiously enough these strictures have come from quarters that have clean overlooked their own federal history. These misunderstandings arise from the same error we recognize from the assessment of democracy as more than a vehicle for public affairs. Federalism is abused in ignorant quarters, (or at least, those in which deliberate misunderstanding serves a political purpose), because it is thought to be an instrument for containing independence instead of being what it is supposed to be, a generally accepted legal method of guaranteeing independence.

In the final analysis, all nations in which races or tribes live peacefully together are the result of some form of federalism. Those places in which the experiment has not yet been attempted, or else where it has been tried, and failed for the time being, are nations not attuned to the requirements of a new era.

The quicker ideas of victors and vanquished are relegated to the sports arena, where they belong, to satisfy the chauvinistic, die-hard streak in all of us, the better. In the forward looking terms of future coexistence, these criteria have no place. Our prosperity is as indivisible as are our hard times. The future of our planet is merely the future of us all.

There, I have had my say. It is now my turn to listen to the many fine minds which have contributed to this book. I am certainly in disagreement with some of them, but that only increases my obligation to listen. Learning only ends with death; if then, depending on the beliefs of the individual.

After so many millania, it is time man learns to live without an enemy

Sir Peter Ustinov

CHAPTER ONE

A MILLION
MINUTES
OF
PEACE

Launching of the Million Minutes of
Peace Appeal, Trafalgar Square,
London, UK

The story of this book begins with three young Australians caught in a traffic jam between Sydney and Canberra in December 1985. With the hot sun of the Australian summer beating down on them, they decided to make use of their enforced inactivity by thinking of ways to contribute to the International Year of Peace (1986) declared by the United Nations.

The question of how that could be done had been broached by the office for the United Nations of the Brahma Kumaris World Spiritual University, an international non-governmental organization to which all three belonged. Committed to the cause of individual peace of mind, as well as the broader objectives of the United Nations, the Brahma Kumaris teach Raja Yoga meditation and had asked their members and students to think of ways to support the International Year of Peace.

The idea born in the Australian traffic jam became the Million Minutes of Peace Appeal, which asked people to pledge to spend time in meditation, positive thinking or prayer for peace. The reasoning was that as people around the world pledged to reflect on peace, they would focus on the fundamental unity of the human spirit and the eternal realities of which all are a part. It would highlight the waste and shallowness of conflict. The Million Minutes project also aimed at giving individuals a sense of participation in dealing with an issue that most people consider quite beyond their power to influence. As one housewife and mother wrote in making her donation of thirty minutes: "Peace has to start as an individual decision. By making a choice to focus even a small segment of my day on peace, I am taking that first step towards every rational person's fantasy - saving the world." (Ophelia Julien, USA)

The project began with the aim of collecting pledges of a million minutes from each participating country, but the response overwhelmed all expectation. In four weeks (mid-September to mid-October 1986) 1,231,975,713 minutes were collected from 88 countries. The total was equal to some 2,344 years of peace! That hefty pledge of popular support for peace was presented to United Nations Secretary-General Javier Perez de Cuellar on 24th October 1986.

Among the initiatives to emerge from the International Year of Peace was the decision by Secretary-General Perez de Cuellar to designate "Peace Messenger" organizations working in support of the United Nations. The Brahma Kumaris World Spiritual University was so designated, and in 1988, as a follow-up to the Million Minutes of Peace Appeal, it undertook a project that came to be called Global Cooperation for a Better World. Essentially, it elicited from people, in words or pictures, responses to the question: What is your vision of a better world? In answering that question, people were asked to observe just one rule, known as the Golden Rule: to couch their replies in positive terms (and not as a negation of anything they disliked).

The Brahma Kumaris, with the invaluable support of many, many friends, advisors, patrons and sponsors, coordinated a world-wide effort to collect visions of a better world. Workshops, conferences, seminars, festivals, dramatic productions and exhibitions were organized. Creative Groups were formed in many parts of the world to share ideas and perspectives. Business and civic leaders, citizens' groups and private individuals volunteered their support. School children in over 20 countries wrote a Global Poem using a world-wide computer link-up. Television monitors at EXPO 88 invited participation by visitors, as did numerous international organizations at their own meetings and conferences. Planned and implemented independently at local community and national levels, these diverse activities provided people with a rare opportunity to participate in a global endeavour. That sharing of common goals and ideals gave people a sense that their thoughts and actions mattered.

A database, the Global Cooperation Bank, was established to receive and store details of all ideas and actions, and in early 1989, when it had input from over 60 countries, National Coordinators prepared a synopsis of the ideas and visions most frequently expressed. These were compiled into a 300 page International Report which was used as the working document for a meeting in February 1989, at the headquarters of the Brahma Kumaris World Spiritual University at Mt. Abu, in the cool hills that rise above India's Rajasthan desert. Project participants representing all parts of the world drew upon the International Report to prepare a one page statement entitled The Peoples' Vision and a set of Principles of Cooperation. Both were incorporated in The Mount Abu Declaration.

The Declaration included a programme of action to articulate a more detailed Global Vision. To that end, project activities expanded to over 120 countries by 1990, aiming specifically to involve professionals, academics and civic leaders in discussing their views of the future.

Depositing a vision in the Global Cooperation Bank. (Greg O'Donnell, Australia)

Students in Brisbane, Australia with Global Poem. (Deborah Voght, Australia)

This was done in two ways. One was through a number of small discussion-groups called Roundtables (of about a dozen members each), involving people of varied expertise and disciplines. Each group developed an in-depth vision statement covering several specific sectors such as science, education, communication, medicine, technology, art, law, business and the environment. The other way was through the distribution of questionnaires, seeking expert responses to The Peoples' Vision and asking people in over 100 countries for their personal visions of the future. Meanwhile, the Mt. Abu Declaration was widely circulated. In September 1989, following its official submission to the United Nations by the Government of Trinidad & Tobago, the Declaration was issued as a General Assembly document (Document A/44/549).

A month after the Global Cooperation Bank was closed to entries in January 1990, a team consisting of project coordinators from all regions of the world assembled, again in Mt. Abu. They produced The Global Vision Statement, synthesizing all materials within the Bank and reflecting contributions of people in over 120 countries.

This book is an effort to reflect some of the vast outpouring of colour and creativity produced by the Global Cooperation project. By necessity, it is only a small sampling, but it is indicative of the whole because of the overview and summary provided by The Global Vision Statement and the careful selection of individual thoughts and visions. Also, despite the uniqueness of personal visions and statements, there is a commonality of ideals and values that makes for an amazing unity cutting across all boundaries of nationality, race and creed. Together, these visions make clear the vital core of our shared humanity, the immutable basis for a world at peace.

It is my deep conviction that every human life is precious and that every human being ought to be able to live his or her life to the fullness of its potential, in harmony and fellowship with other human beings, and in partnership with nature. I am equally convinced that we have at our disposal the intellectual, material and moral resources to bring about such a result. To succeed in such a quest requires that we emphasize the things that unite us as human beings and build on the foundations of shared values and common concern for human welfare.

The starting point for action is a vision of the oneness of humankind and of the world that can be established through mutual care, solidarity and cooperation. Once there is shared belief that such a world is possible, its realization will become a matter of method and of effort. Hence, the double significance of vision: first to paint the future, and second to delineate the paths to be followed for getting there.

When my views were first sought about the launching of this project, following the successful "Million Minutes of Peace" project, the idea caught my imagination. I enthusiastically supported the inauguration of the project, with the knowledge that, for centuries,

A dance for the world at the launch of Global Cooperation at the Conservatoire
Rachmaninov, Paris, France. (Sophie Guerbadot, France)

there had been a debate whether the individual could play a role in
determining world conditions and in affecting issues of war and peace.
While not minimizing the importance of leadership, I have always felt
that the individual has a specific role to play.

Recent developments in the world have once more demonstrated
that individuals, when determined and cooperating, can bring about
radical changes in the human condition. This is the faith that has
motivated me in this project. As I travelled in many parts of the
world in favour of the project and saw the way that individuals of
different races and backgrounds have been motivated, I became
convinced even more about the wisdom of such a project. It is not
enough that we listen to world leaders alone about their visions of the
world. It is of enormous value to learn how ordinary individuals,
regardless of age or background, view the world and also to learn
about their visions. Such visions may initially appear naive or utopian,
but one can learn from them and they may be the deciding factor in
bringing about a radical change in the conduct of human affairs.
Such individual visions are often made without the constraints that
can influence the vision and conduct of world leaders.

The compilation of visions of the world undoubtedly serves a
useful purpose not only in giving a total picture of how people in
different walks of life feel, but also in showing clearly where they
converge on the crucial issues of global peace.

These visions and ideas, expressed by people of diverse ages,
backgrounds and cultures, carry a common message and I sincerely
hope that they will help point the way to a better world.

When I think of global vision, of the oneness of humanity and of the boundless potential of joint action for human welfare, the stirring lines of the poet Tagore come to my mind:

"Where the mind is without fear and the head is held high;
Where knowledge is free;
Where the world has not been broken up into fragments by
narrow domestic walls;
Where words come out from the depth of truth;
Where tireless striving stretches its arms towards perfection;
Where the clear stream of reason has not lost its way into the dreary
desert sand of dead habit;
Where the mind is led forward by thee into ever-widening
thought and action -
Into that heaven of freedom, my father, let [the world] awake."

James O. C. Jonah, Under-Secretary-General, United Nations
Co-Chairman, International Advisory Commitee, Global Cooperation for a Better World

A crowd of over 12,000 Adiwasis (indigenous people of India) at a Global Cooperation function; Jagdalpur, India.(B.K. Ramesh, India)

CHAPTER TWO

HOW
TO USE
THIS BOOK

Global Cooperation's float in the annual Moomba Festival in Melbourne, Australia, won first prize in the community section. (Yaja Nowakowski, Australia)

In part, this book is a report on a programme of mass involvement in thinking about a better world. It is, however, also a manual for personal involvement in building a better world. The reader will find many ideas about how to do that in this book, but if there is one that subsumes all others, it is that people must think of the future actively, in terms of their own lives. Each person is a seed of the better world, gifted with the power to grow and change. The process of saving the world must begin with each of us accepting the responsibility for our own improvement.

To think, to hope and to dream are abilities enjoyed by people throughout the world, regardless of culture, gender, race or social status. In improving ourselves - and thus the world - the first step is to recognize the unbreakable links between our inner world of ideas, thoughts and concepts, and the external world of event and circumstance. Just because our world today is so changeable and volatile is no reason for despair. Quite the contrary, for the reason why we now live in a world that is changing more rapidly than at any time before in human history, is precisely because individuals have unprecedented power.

It is human ingenuity that has brought the world into the current era of great technological advancement. Everything that we have created, from the clothes we wear to the satellites in the sky, had its origin in the human mind. If we forget that, we are likely to endow them with an impersonal power of their own, beyond the control of our own minds and will. It is important to remember always that the machines, artifacts and other inventions that human beings have made are only instruments to be used as we choose. Thus a syringe can be used to inject dangerous addictive drugs or lifesaving vaccines; aircraft can be used for travel to promote friendship and understanding or to wage war; the power within the atom can be used to release energy for overall human development or mass destruction.

Everything depends on our power of choice. In making those choices, our decisions will be sound to the extent that we are guided by a sense of integrity, conscience and responsibility.

Every person has inherent worth, regardless of race, sex, religion, nationality or culture. This is so because every individual is a unique creation of that universal power we call God. Material differences such as those that spring from affluence or poverty, education, social status and political authority, are all of little consequence in the face of the basic underlying equality of all men and women.

In practical terms, some may have a lesser or greater impact on the world but that does not alter the fact that each individual contributes to the state of affairs in the world in some way, and none need be without power in dealing with the terms of his or her own reality.

Canon Lloyd Casson re-building the world at the International Conference on Global Cooperation at Mt. Abu, India.
(B.K. Ramesh, India)

That personal power can be exercised in thought, an energy that knows no barriers and can be truly controlled by none but the thinker. In our world today there are many distractions to thought, many factors that tend to limit its use or channel it in particular ways. This is especially true of situations of conflict. The first step towards liberation from these factors comes with our recognition of them, and of our inherent ability to go beyond them, for the awakened consciousness is the root of all attempts to deal with the realities we face.

In the pages that follow, people from countries around the world testify to this truth in remarkably varied ways. To use this book to its best advantage, it must not merely be read. The reader must imagine the reality that inspires each quotation, for there is behind each one a person, a life, a unique vitality. Each thought in this book may be reflected upon, separately, carefully. Lift each quotation to the light of your own thought and experience, and you will see how, like a fine jewel catching the sun, it will flash with sudden brilliance.

The Better World starts with each one of us; we are all the seeds of a better world

Every sportsman or woman needs the power of vision to see themselves achieving the pinnacle of their particular sport. Those who have such a mental attitude, fulfil their dreams in practical.

Perhaps it's the same with the world. When individuals create their highest vision of a Better World then the reality of cooperation, understanding and unity can come close.

Without dreams the world would stand still! Let's dream together.

Max Walker, Television Sports Presenter, Australia

The problems we face today - violent conflicts, destruction of nature, poverty, hunger and so on - are mainly problems created by humans. They can be resolved - but only through human effort, understanding and the development of a sense of brotherhood and sisterhood. To do this we need to cultivate a universal responsibility for one another and for the planet we share based on a good heart and awareness.

H. H. The Dalai Lama

I always believed in a better world but nobody shared this with me, until I came across Global Cooperation. Then I realized that my feelings and ideas had deep significance. I no longer thought I was an idealist or a dreamer; suddenly I came across the people whom I had always wanted to meet. From now on, I dedicate all my art for the creation of a better world and I shall only paint for a better world.

Eva Castel, Painter, Argentina

Painters working together to portray their vision of a better world during "A Planetary Re-creation" in Paris, France. (Marie Binder, France)

Each citizen is the most important one, because that citizen may be the one more needed to make a difference. It is a big step to know and accept that I am an important link in the creation of world peace. The purpose of this vision is to give every citizen the opportunity to take that one step that will positively contribute to world peace.

Doyar Onye Harry, Civil Servant, Nigeria

Drawing a better world. (G.B. Jarman, Australia)

In his song "Man in the Mirror", Michael Jackson sings that if you want to change the world, you should start with the one you see in the mirror. Well, that is what I am trying to do and I hope everyone will do this and that people do not think that just by themselves they cannot achieve anything. I would like to live in a world where people treat each other like human beings and not just old rags. A world in which nobody is tortured. A peaceful world is my ideal. I hope this will come true one day.

Titia Maas, Student, Age 14, Netherlands

My vision of a better world is one in which the principles of love become a universal way of life, where basic human rights such as freedom, joy, dignity, growth, work, creativity, food and shelter, beauty and happiness are assured to all humankind.

I am not impatient for this wonderful world. It would be sufficient for me to know that each one of us, in some way, is doing something concrete towards achieving these goals, now.

Leo F. Buscaglia, Author, USA

The past cannot be changed, it has left its teachings. The present is the moment to act but it is the future that will direct us where to go. If there is no clarity regarding the future we will be entangled in the problems of the present, of the present that we constructed in the past and which we cannot modify. This is why we must visualize the

Dances at launch of Global Cooperation in Mombasa, Kenya.

future. What is the scene that we, as designers, want to create? How do we interact with the environment in that scene? How do we relate to one another? How do we visualize industry and commerce? How do we behave? The answers will awaken our optimism and with this attitude we will have clarity in our actions now. So the method of transformation is detached observation and visualization of the future.

Vivien Von Son, Industrial Designer, Mexico

Particularly in view of the avant-garde scientific knowledge acquired in recent years and in course of deeper elaboration, we believe that the power of collective thought, when "guided" can bring about incredible transformation. For materialistic pragmatics all of that is impossible. Their restrictive vision of reality stops their imagination, the real power of transformation and creation. But we researchers of the mysteries of consciousness believe that it is only consciousness that can develop order and harmony if it is placed in a capacity to act collectively within a background of harmonious interpretation of the laws of nature.

Professor Dario Schena Sterza, Physicist, Italy

A gigantic fire broke out in the jungle. The animals flocked together on the other side of the lake and they gazed at the flames. A small bird, seeing what was going on, took a drop of water in its little beak and let it drop on the flames. It returned, took another little drop in its beak and let it fall. And like this it flew back and forth diligently. The rest of the animals just watched him and said to each other: "and does this one think he can actually do something with his little drop of water?" At one stage they asked him: "tell us, little bird, do you honestly believe you can put out the fire with your little drop of water?" The little bird answered: "I do what I must". Just then an Angel went by, saw the little bird and produced a great rainfall. The fire went out.

Henny Trailes, Actress, Argentina

There are so many schemes to make this world a better place to live in, schemes on a regional basis, schemes on a national basis, schemes on a global basis. I feel, though, that all these excellent and so necessary schemes will eventually come to nothing, if people do not start changing their way of behaviour in their everyday lives.

Is it really so difficult to smile and say "please" and "thank you", when you ask one of your family to pass the salt, instead of muttering "salt" and grabbing the salt-cellar? I do not think so. And is it really so difficult to smile and say "good morning" to the bus driver before you pay your fare, instead of slamming down your money and mumbling the name of the bus stop you want to go to? It is not.

A bit of politeness, of friendliness, a moment shared in a smile, a word of greeting does not cost anything - quite the contrary: they make your life richer. It is so much easier to be friendly than to be gruff, to smile than to sulk.

Christina L. Griffiths, Administrator, Germany

Reaching for the world at the Global Cooperation Stand at Marjolaine Fair, Paris, France. (Francois Becher, France)

"Smile! It costs nothing!", Claire Reid, Age 15, UK

VISIONS OF A BETTER WORLD

Hato Petera College Performance Group, at North Harbour Fun Festival, Auckland, New Zealand. (Bill Andrew, New Zealand)

People may think they can't do much as individuals, but I don't believe that's true. I might not be able to stop wars and famines or do much to improve the environment, but I can do a lot with my inner environment, like changing my attitudes towards others. I could look at the positive sides of people and situations. I could say nice things about people or I won't say anything at all (I call this "monitoring my mouth") and I won't let nasty comments get me down. Last of all I will control my anger against people and try to be more understanding.

If we did this it would spread throughout our families and then to communities and then to greater populations (maybe even the governments!)

If everyone did this we would have instant heaven on earth.

Sarah Pittwood, Student, Australia

As managing director of the Body Shop in Hong Kong, a business well known for its concern for people and the environment, I was attracted by Global Cooperation's concept that everything starts with the self. Very often the individual is not aware of the power he/she can wield. Together we have the power of a group, and groups have the power of a multitude. So it is very true that one person can change the world! It is never too late to change. The smallest thing can change people. It is a question of getting people's awareness to change and you can do that in a number of ways.

Workshops were conducted in English and Cantonese to prepare staff for various community activities. We then linked up with Helping Hand, a relief organization caring for the elderly, and staff members are given half a day off each month to visit senior citizens. Other spin-offs were an environmental workshop which attracted prominent business personalities, politicians and community leaders, a Green Symposium promoting environmental protection and community programmes serving vulnerable children and the mentally handicapped.

All this has affected other people's awareness and made them think how they can help. Already another company has offered its staff half a day off each month for community projects. As consumers we have real power to effect change. However huge and distant the problem may seem, we all have some small part to play in the solution of it. We believe that YOU, the individual, are one crucial factor in determining the fate of the global environment.

Margaret Tancock, Managing Director, Body Shop, Hong Kong

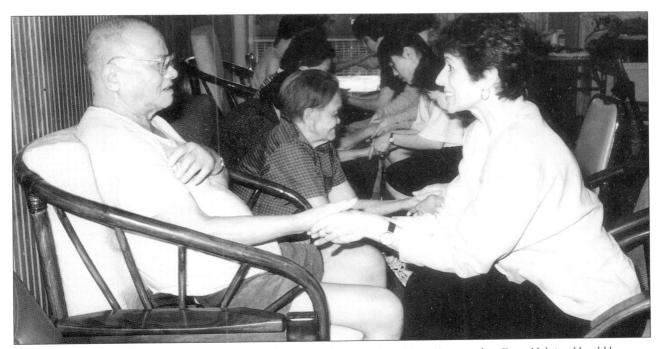

"Helping Hands" - Ms. Margaret Tancock, Managing Director, The Body Shop, Hong Kong, and staff at a Helping Hand Home for the Elderly. (Maureen Chen, Hong Kong)

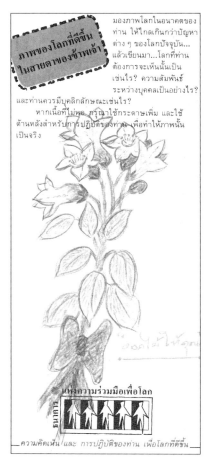

ภาพของโลกที่ดีขึ้น
ในสายตาของข้าพเจ้า

มองภาพโลกในอนาคตของ
ท่าน ให้ไกลเกินกว่าปัญหา
ต่าง ๆ ของโลกปัจจุบัน...
แล้วเขียนมา...โลกที่ท่าน
ต้องการจะเห็นนั้นเป็น
เช่นไร? ความสัมพันธ์
ระหว่างบุคคลเป็นอย่างไร?
และท่านควรมีบุคลิกลักษณะเช่นไร?
หากเนื้อที่ไม่พอ กรุณาใช้กระดาษเพิ่ม และใช้
ด้านหลังสำหรับการปฏิบัติของท่าน เพื่อทำให้ภาพนั้น
เป็นจริง

"Flowers for You", drawn on Global
Cooperation participation form,
Patchara Lumubol, Thailand.

My vision is that the human race is evolving from the stage of self-centred to whole-centred or God-centred consciousness. At some point, perhaps within our life time, there will be a critical mass of consciousness that knows we are connected to each other, to nature and to the whole creation. A mass global mind change will occur.

Barbara Marx Hubbard, Author/Futurist, USA

The atmosphere at work was predominantly negative and it had become "fashionable" to criticize colleagues. All discussions tended to drift into this pattern. I have to confess that, almost without realizing it, I had allowed myself to get caught up in this trend. There was a certain superficial satisfaction in hearing people say "Have you heard what so-and-so has done now?" and thinking "Aren't I clever, I would never do anything so stupid". But it was a very superficial satisfaction, and underneath I was feeling increasingly uncomfortable about it.

Then one day it dawned on me that I didn't have to go along with it, and that if MY attitude was more positive, things might change. Instead of thinking "I could get on with so-and-so if he/she were reasonable", I said to myself "What if I were more reasonable?"

Having got this far and realizing that I wanted to change, I thought to myself "Now, where do I start?" One day, on the spur of the moment, I invited an "unreasonable" colleague to coffee. He accepted with an alacrity which surprised me and didn't stop talking for 20 minutes! I realized afterwards that he was someone who needed to have that sort of social contact with his colleagues, and he became much easier to work with afterwards. The coffee sessions still continue and have been extended to include other colleagues. Now there is a greater feeling of working together as a team instead of looking for someone to criticize. If criticism does arise, I greet it with silence - it does not survive long on that diet.

Charmian Common, Technical Assistant, Switzerland

How can we develop an optimal model of the future world and create one where most people would be happier than they are today? Is it possible? I believe that scientifically acquired knowledge of the laws and mechanisms underlying the functioning of the human brain can contribute to an understanding of some social laws, and hence to people's well-being on this planet.

From prehistoric man to our contemporary one every individual tries to solve his everyday and every year tasks by relying on the abilities of his brain. As it is the brain which has created society I propose that we take into account certain data on brain mechanisms when considering the individual or events in society.

If a long lasting, so-called chronic illness develops in man, it is his adaptation to his surroundings which will permit him to survive in these new conditions. This involves the formation of a new stable state, or in medical terminology, stable pathological state. Medical literature mentions that the treatment to achieve such a new stable state can include any such influences which help bring about the transition of the brain (and the whole body as well) into a new stable state.

It is not unusual that states closer to the normal one are achieved not through smooth improvement but through phases of destabilization. This is not always the case but a possibility which we met when investigating brain mechanisms and treating brain diseases. Nevertheless, this mechanism can be analyzed and used as a model in situations when trying to help optimize the state of a "sick" society. What we would like to stress here is that "normalization" of a "sick" society can sometimes be achieved only through phases of instability and that only a properly oriented course of "treatment" brings about the new and desired stability. This can be the case even if the "treatment" is planned from above, by the government.

The possibilities of a human brain are enormous. However this is only true when certain necessary conditions are fulfilled; the brain has to be in an optimal state which permits use of all its abilities. Some few years ago I dealt with this very problem in relation to the nuclear threat. The paper was published in the book "Breakthrough". Some passages of this paper can be brought up here. Our brain, when functioning properly, has the creative capacity to produce solutions for plenty of problems.

Careful studies of the human brain have demonstrated the power of sustained negative emotions, such as fear of approaching disaster, to "unbalance" the brain's normal state. An imbalance causes the brain's electrical levels to rise too high or fall too low. When that happens, a person can become either excessively excited on the one hand (close to "mental breakdown") or emotionally shut down on the other (emotionally dull or numb). This robs the individual of the ability fully to respond to situations in life and also robs society of that person's creative potential at a time when great creativity is needed to avoid devastation.

The essential point is that our minds have a potential flexibility and richness in order to maintain abilities of thought and emotion but, to realize maximal capability, each of the brain's zones must be in an optimal functional state.

There is always a certain level of slowly changing physiological activity in each zone, a small voltage called the "steady potential." Our clinical work demonstrates that when the steady potential for any brain zone becomes too high or too low, that area of the brain either fails to act or its capacities for action drastically diminish. The rich endowment of the brain is lost. It may have to concentrate all of its energy to be able to maintain just one activity. There is a gradual hampering of all the complex processes associated with the thought process as well. The creativity of the human brain decreases dramatically.

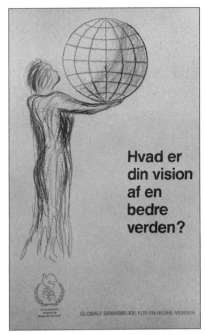

"Give Your Playground a Lift", Global Cooperation Project Poster, Solveig Ellegard Poulsen, Denmark.

VISIONS OF A BETTER WORLD

The laboratory data are quite clear. As a patient having a strong fear episode brings his or her fear under control, one can watch on a recorder reciprocal shifts of the steady potential of the brain and later its return to previous levels.

If these conditions of over-excitement and emotional numbing are allowed to happen in a large number of human beings, and our intelligentsia, humanity will see a significant decline in the planet's creative potential. One can visualize this as a sort of "scissor" graph. The ascending line of the graph is the growth of the planet's creative potential in connection with the ever growing increase in the pool of knowledge. The descending line, on the other hand, is the degeneration of humanity's creative potential because of the impact of the knowledge of our impending doom. The degeneration can possibly outweigh the potential creativity, thus robbing the planet of its creative potential, a unique and most precious treasure. Creativity is needed now more than ever and must be reoriented to the task of preserving humanity as well as all other life on our planet.

Natalia P. Bechtereva, Brain Scientist, St. Petersburg, Russia

I enjoin all Filipinos to participate in this laudable project which provides an opportunity and a method for people to come together, in small groups, to change human values and create a better world.

The Philippines donated 94 million minutes of prayers, thoughts and meditations on the occasion of the International Year of Peace.

Now let us, as individuals, families, and organizations, work together to create our vision of a better world through positive ideas and actions.

I hope that through this and similar initiatives we shall achieve lasting peace in our land.

Corazon C. Aquino, Philippines

CHAPTER THREE

THE VALUE OF THE SELF

"Searching for the Light",
Ana Maria Ferrer, Spain

For the majority of the world's people, life is a struggle. Many millions are afflicted by the basic deprivations of poverty, disease, and hunger, by crime, drug addiction, unemployment, physical and mental abuse, war and natural calamities. Despite these dark circumstances, people keep going. They not only survive, they often laugh in the face of adversity. They sing and dance, create art, write poetry, love each other, raise children, and express in thousands of ways the indomitable human spirit.

Philosophers and spiritual leaders over the ages have pointed out that this is possible only because life has a reality that goes beyond all that is physical. Those who experience this transcendence know that the value of the self, or the sanctity of the soul, is not derived from the circumstances of the world. It has little to do with economic, social or political eminence. Religions, official Declarations, Conventions and other legal instruments cannot confer this worth; all they can do is acknowledge it and highlight its importance.

Those who are out of touch with transcendent reality cannot forge a conscious link with God, the Supreme Spirit, and Source of all that is good. In our moral universe, these are the people capable of Evil, who by thought and deed commit violence against their own innate worth, that of their fellow human beings and nature. In this context, one becomes a force for good by developing one's innate abilities with integrity, which is to say, by remaining true to the ultimate goodness inherent within, by retaining respect for the self and for others. Integrity is a quality essential in making the right choices in life, no matter what the circumstances may be.

Human Worth - the silent truth within

Worldly fears and tears
Vanish among serene hills
Silence, my soul hears

Glendale G. Yap, Manager, Philippines

To bring about a better world therefore, each of us must know our worth, our potential, and the power of our thoughts. If our present civilization is to survive the stress and strain of mental and moral decay, we in this generation must catch a vision of a better world, and will that better world into being.

Eugenia Springer, Human Relations Consultant, Trinidad & Tobago

Robin Ramsay as Rabindranath Tagore in "Borderland", a celebration of the life of Tagore, which toured world-wide in favour of Global Cooperation. (Jon Russell, Australia)

We rely very much on our feelings about ourselves as a reference point in order to make decisions. This wouldn't be a problem if our feelings themselves had not been contorted. When you are brought up from the year dot in a completely crazy situation, where your parents have split up, the police behave in a manner inconsistent with "serve and protect" which is written on the side of their car, and so on, it probably stands to reason that your feelings are pretty messed up too. And so here you are thinking I can't trust anybody's words so I'm going to trust how I feel but you have been taught to feel violent thoughts. Your family situation, school conditions, T.V., social habits and surroundings, have taught you to react in a particular way to certain standard stimuli. So it is as though the ultimate con job has been played on you. You can't trust what anyone says and you can't trust what you feel so what are you meant to do? And this is where in discovering the true meaning of worth and integrity, this notion of silence comes in. Somewhere in the sea of the mind and in the sea of experience there is calm; somewhere in there, if we are awake enough, perhaps we can catch a glimpse of the truth.

Anthony Phelips, Advertising Executive, Canada

Original project participation form, which reads, "I will try to get in closer contact with other people - to experience them more intensely and find a way to the core in each person I meet, without asking about age, sex, profession, nationality, colour, income, education etc". Lina Dupont, Denmark

I had decided that I wanted to go to South Africa. This prompted me to do something I had been meaning to do for a while, which was to change my passport into a British one. This was a simple procedure but suddenly I found that a whole new dimension opened up as countries in Europe and South America that had questioned my entry before were now very happy to accept me. I don't think that I had changed in the few days it took to get the new passport but the acquiring of this new passport made all that difference to the immigration officials where I was travelling. This is an example of a factor that seems very greatly to determine the apparent value of a human being.

Jayanti Kirpalani, Teacher, UK

It's important to keep your head cool. I was quite a quick-tempered person by nature, so that is something I really had to learn. Formerly, when I disagreed with someone, I put my back into it and walked over everybody. Even if I was right, I acted so emotionally that nobody would listen. Now I know much better how to see things in their proper perspective, take some distance and consciously lead my thoughts in a different direction. As a consequence people take me more seriously. I try to respect people, whether they are criminals, foreigners or whoever. They are humans the same as anyone else. The other day I met a boy who I know plays fast and loose with the law. We get on well, and when I asked him how things were going, he said: "Alright, still a criminal". That's fine with me. I always try to work in a pleasant way with other people. As a consequence people who work with me feel at ease, for that's how it works. I believe life is something to be created. This job involves you in a lot of misery. At a certain point you can't help protecting yourself against it. It hardens

"Sun, Moon and Stars", Montessori Normal Distrital Maria, Colombia

"Move, Cloud…Move!", a scene from "Kalpa", a youth musical dedicated to Global Cooperation, Tokyo, Japan. (Brian Young, Japan)

you. I notice this in many of my colleagues: their world gets smaller and smaller, they become more and more narrow-minded. That sort of thing is very unpleasant and partly for that reason some colleagues and I followed a course of positive thinking. Not everyone appreciates a positive attitude to life. Some say it's soft. My answer is then you don't know the meaning of positivity. I think it is very powerful. Getting to know one's own qualities makes one stand firm in one's shoes. That is the opposite of being soft, isn't it?

Walter Teekamp, Police Sergeant, Netherlands

It is essential that we use part of our leisure time for "quiet time". Time in which we think and evaluate ourselves and look into ourselves so that we can work on ourselves and become better people.

Jaclyn Piudik, Fashion Photographer, Israel

Dennis Weaver talking about Global Cooperation at Griffith Park Boys' Club, Los Angeles, California, USA. (Joan N. Derry, USA)

Love is the most powerful force in the universe. No chasm so wide that enough love will not bridge. No hate so cold that enough love will not melt. No greed so entrenched that enough love will not dissolve and no ignorance so dark that enough love will not enlighten. We are not powerless for we have the power of choice, the power to love and the power to think.

Dennis Weaver, Actor, USA

There are many characteristics inborn in all of us that carry on into early childhood, such as honesty, loyalty, trust and being loving. As children, we could be trusted not to lie, cheat or steal, never to betray another person and to love one another openly. However, as we grow older, some of these inborn traits fade, and somehow we are transformed from innocent children into corrupted adults. My better world? That we not lose the characteristics that we are born with, that we not allow ourselves to be taken over by hate, guilt, fear and pride. If we try to keep our "childlike" ways, then perhaps this would be a better world.

Lea Salonga, Actress/Singer, Philippines

One more remark on what a person is: A person is like a ship on the sea, this is because every ship has its day to sink and so we see that a person might be very active and also young but when time comes he becomes old and drowns like a ship.

Rajeev K. Khagram, Student, Age 15, Kenya

I believe that it is intrinsic to human nature to have an inner light which makes you see things clearly in your heart. Even if they have had no education or no experience there are some things which every human being knows and can judge clearly.

Aureliano Tello, Diplomat, Chile

The interconnectedness of everything on earth, of peoples between each other, of nations, even of men and women together, is the most important issue. This interconnectedness is really what has to save us and if people and governments do not see this interconnectedness, if they separate it and are not thinking spiritually, then I think we will lose the battle to save the earth and to save ourselves. We have to believe in ourselves. You, yourself can make a change. You, yourself have the problems and the solutions in you. Each person can make a very powerful difference. We have to believe in our own strengths. Governments tend to feel that people are powerless and we tend to feel powerless but if you believe that you can really be transforming something and also transform yourself then that is the first step towards changing the world.

Petra Kelly, Germany

I think the human being is fundamentally inclined to good. I think that man has been corrupted, not by birth but by exposure to his environment, so ultimately I have faith that the individual can distinguish between good and bad and therefore can make the right choices. Ultimately you are appealing to the mind and conscience of the human being and I myself have great faith in that. Man can be awakened by all sorts of realizations and I think you perhaps need to stimulate his instincts and appeal to his reason. I don't see why the process of degradation cannot be halted in most cases - once you are persuasive enough I think man can be brought back on the straight and narrow. In a way it is like going to one's roots, after having gone astray.

Samuel R. Insanally, Ambassador, Guyana

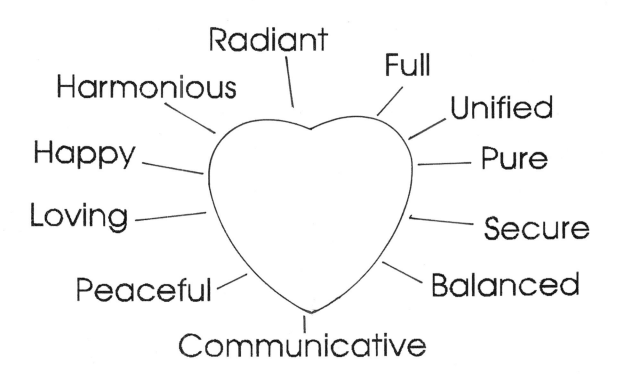

"The true self", Creative Group, Argentina

CHAPTER FOUR

THE GLOBAL VISION

A Gift to the World from the People of the World

"Offering", Marie Binder, France

"My World", Lisa Le Gresley, Age 12, UK

THE GLOBAL VISION STATEMENT

In a better world:

1. All people celebrate the joy of life.

2. Human Rights are respected and upheld and the dignity and integrity of all people is assured.

3. People live in ways that preserve nature's ecological balance in an environment that is beautiful and clean.

4. The planet's natural and abundant resources are shared equitably and the basic human needs of all people are provided for.

5. All people have equal opportunities to realize their potential through an educational process that has human, moral and spiritual values at its heart.

6. Life within the immediate family is loving, caring and fulfilling and is the foundation for harmony within the broader human family.

7. There is respect, understanding and tolerance in all human relations.

8. People communicate openly and in a spirit of equality and goodwill.

9. Social, economic and political justice is ensured through honesty, responsibility and respect for the rule of law.

10. Governments, as representatives of their people, are committed to their well-being. People participate cooperatively in efforts for a secure and peaceful world.

11. Science serves humanity and appropriate technology is applied to ensure sustainable development and enhance the quality of life.

12. All people enjoy freedom of expression, movement and belief while respecting the liberties and rights of others.

Imagine a vision that carries the authority of the will and the voice of people from the East, the West, the North and the South - a vision born from the ideals and inspirations of men, women and children who dare to dream and have the courage to live by their commitment to that dream.

We all know the things that we don't want to see in the world - we don't want disease, wars, high taxes or pollution - but are we really so sure of the kind of world we do want? Hundreds of thousands of individuals all over the world participated in the Global Cooperation project by sharing their hopes and aspirations for the future with project coordinators. The Global Vision Statement is a synthesis of these hopes and now stands as a testimony of what a better world means to people in over 120 countries. As a framework of the principles by which people want to live, it calls for a way of life in which daily actions are based upon fundamental and universally identified human and moral values. Numbered for ease of reference only, and not to indicate any particular order of priority, each point of the Statement is featured on the following pages with samples of the international array of visions from which it was derived.

"ALL GREAT ACHIEVEMENTS AND CHANGES START WITH A VISION."

As a youngster I dreamt of being the fastest bowler in the world and the best of this kind. If for a time I may have been close to being this then it may have been due to having been blessed with a good measure of talent for sport and what I have been told by others was a high degree of application and will to succeed.

Without doubt the greatest thrills I experienced in sport were from being a part of an improving team. The sharing was exciting and the encouragement each received from others was exhilarating. Whilst we may not all have the potential to be intellectuals or sportsmen of the highest order we all have the potential to be people of the highest principles and character.

Let us combine these three ideas. Let us share a vision of a better world where values of the highest order prevail and genuine concern for each other and true cooperation are realities. We need to strive with unyielding determination towards a world that encourages the development of the spiritual aspect of our being and the peace and understanding that accompanies this. How very exciting is the idea of the people of the world forming a huge team that has the vision and would apply itself with great purpose and determination to change humanity for the good.

All great achievements and changes start with a vision.

Dennis Lillee, Company Director, Australia

Dance of the Nations, by Ballet Dalal Achcar, Rio de Janeiro, Brazil. (Adelino Augusto V. Santos, Brazil)

"Long Live Peace in the World", Mdm. Chiang Yu Tie, Indonesia

In a Better World:

All people celebrate the joy of life.

人人享受生活的欢乐。

Человечество торжествует радость жизни.

Chacun manifeste avec allégresse sa joie de vivre.

يحتفل الناس جميعا· ببهجة الحياة

Todas las personas celebran la alegría de vivir.

1 THE JOY OF LIFE

We are the flowers of a single garden,
The fruits of a single tree,
And the waves of one sea.

Visitor to Global Cooperation
"Art for a better world" exhibition
at 1989 Marseille International Fair, France

There is an intimate dialogue between the mother and child. The arrival of the child is like a celebration.

Roundtable Group, France

Differences between people are a cause for celebration.

Brenda Markland, Doctor, Canada

Children of a better world should be allowed to run, sing, dance and shout wherever and whenever they want to...

Euripedes Alcantara, Editor, Brazil

Let us look at a football game. It can attract the entire world's attention. It makes people happy. The ball belongs to all, both the player and the watcher. But no one realizes that the globe belongs to them, that it is for them to take care of. Why can't we see how God moves it through the cycle of day and night.

Karmin Mohammed Elairashi, Student, Jordan

Life is a game and one enjoys it!

Creative Group, Netherlands

In a better world I would like to:
    live in peace
    respect elder people
    have a very big house with beautiful furniture
    go in a mercedes benz when going to school
    look very handsome
    be a clever child
    have very rich parents
    have many friends at school, home and everywhere
    live happily and eat good food.

Webster Nzala, Age 14, Zambia

Life is a major work of art.

Jose William Soledad Espindola, Colombia

"Peaceful Environment and Harmony Between Man and Nature", Sheetal Shah and Reezwan Popat, Age 12, Kenya

If we had a perfect world
There would be lots of fun!
There would be love
And plenty for everyone!!
Justin Jagai, Age 9, Trinidad & Tobago

I am flying above the earth. Flying
unnoticed. How beautiful my planet is!
It is a garden in full bloom. Human
beings are beautiful. How kind and
bright their faces are, how much
harmony is in their souls! Their smiles
are presenting everybody with joy.
Everyone is a creator, and works
enthusiastically. I see laughing children
and I'm laughing with them. Beauty
saved the world.

Kirill Evgenyevich Rodov, Student, Russia

In this future world I would be a
very sweet person, full of contentment
and always ready to help the ones close
to me. I would always be at peace with
myself and with others; I would be full of
inspiration, enthusiasm and love.
Maria Raquel da C. M. Carreira,
Housewife, Portugal

I want to see a world where everyone is a brother or a sister to each other.
A world where inner joy is felt and
lived.

Joseph Koffi, Draftsman, Cote d'Ivoire

"The Awakening", Angelica Landreani, Argentina

It would be ideal for all human beings to enjoy a peaceful spirit, a happy mind and a healthy body, but
not all of us know or want to know about these gifts given to us from the Supreme Being, so that we can live
according to his plan.

Ines and Maria Moscal Tobar, Ecuador

Creativity, imagination and good dreaming would be celebrated. Life would be fun.

Alan Tuckett, Director, UK

The goal of living is happiness.

Amos Nazael Madalla, Lecturer, Tanzania

"People's Happiness in the World", Raquel Romero Jerez, Spain

Hello and how do you do?
How's the world a treatin' you?
I hope you're fine
'Cos I am.
And the world?
Why it's a beautiful place.
Smile and be happy
Cos' life is too short
To be a-cryin' all the time
So smile and be happy.

D. Suvarna, Teacher, Kenya

Since childhood I always believed that life was divine, a unique, true miracle: to see the stars, the sky, the marvels of the Earth and to meet people was a source of endless wonders. Therefore the idea of wars, of "miracles" killing or hurting each other was horrendous to me. God allowed me to work all my life for that belief.

Robert Muller, Chancellor, University for Peace, France

There is a wonder house found in the hearts of the children which fulfills all their secret hopes and dreams. Children would be allowed to be themselves in an environment which is clean and pure and free from fearsome experiences, a place where they can feel totally safe. There would be full freedom to play, to develop their abilities and to make full use of their fantasy. The relationship between children and adults would be close and natural. Adults would still be aware of the little children within themselves and thereby adults and children would be able to meet each other on an equal level.

Rolf Hagen, Artist, Sweden

I feel there should be great respect for all living beings: humans, animals and the surrounding nature.

Aloi Pilioko, Painter, Vanuatu

Let's all be brothers for this better world giving a hand to the ones who do not have, telling them: come with me, I will help you; we will fill their eyes with light and this better world will bring them the gift of the smile of life.

Montserrat Caballe, Singer, Spain

"Life", Angelica Landreani, Argentina

In my vision the world is tranquil, calm and full of peace.

Chamlong Srimuang, Member of Parliament, Thailand

In that world I will be serene, self-confident, clear-eyed and full of faith and hope.

Pamela O'Cuneen, Writer, Swaziland

We feel happy, lighthearted and carefree. Our activities are joyous, running along the soft green grass, skipping, spinning around with happy, smiling faces. The gentle breeze blows through our long-flowing hair. With a feeling of total satisfaction and contentment we bathe, splash and swim in blue pools of sparkling, crystal clear, perfumed water, then we play with the little deer that drink from the pools.

Roundtable Group, Trinidad & Tobago

The world is a field and we
are born to cultivate the field.
Once we learn to cultivate the field
we can produce anything.
Love for our brothers is the rent
we pay for our room in the hereafter.
Love is the net where
hearts are caught like fish.

Mohammed Ali, USA

Traditional dances at a Global Cooperation function for Adiwasis; Jagdalpur, India (B.K. Ramesh, India)

I am dreaming of a world where nobody feels something is missing, where people are like notes out of one song, every note has its own sound on a never-ending theme of human peace and friendship.

I am dreaming of a world where everything becomes smaller to the size of man, full of skills and little shops, where joy fills every house and we rediscover human warmth, where one laughs in the streets, where the healthy and weak, handicapped, young and old, can host each other again and give each other comfort.

I am dreaming of a world where the rich renounce their richness to find their heart again, where human values have priority, where there is space for the song of nature, for a fair and a fanfare, a joke teller and a clown, where people can be happy with a happiness that is free.

I am dreaming of a world with a human face, the face of love!

Phil Bosmans, Belgium

The key to life is the gift of love. The choice is ours, let's follow the dove.

Belinda Dimech, Australia

Easily, so easily, we move through time, enjoying each breath, each new experience and holding on to nothing, for that would detract from the joy of the next moment. Time is as soft as silk drifting by, its pattern ever changing, blending and developing, and always bringing new things. There is no real conception of time itself, just a feeling of the rhythm of life's cycles and the deep underlying awareness that beneath all lies immortality...we know we're all on a journey together and that death has no meaning.

Rachel Flower, Teacher, Thailand

Art opens our eyes, hones our senses, destroys our obfuscating vision of negativism, smashes barriers of despotism, prejudice, malice, greed and escorts us through journeys of contemplative thought. It must be a salient, valuable and contributory aspect of the entire vision for global unity and unification, of brotherly love and tranquility. It must be the cementing factor that binds the human race and transcends all boundaries of status, race, colour and politics. Art then is the essence of order and harmony.

Willi Chen, Artist, Trinidad & Tobago

Human beings are different but all share an appreciation of the unique gift of life. No one has the right to take it away from us.

Najib Bensonda, Travel Agent, Morocco

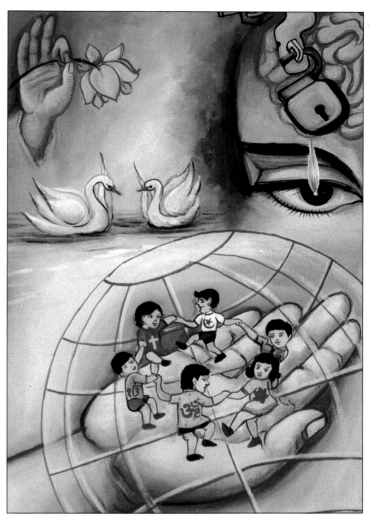

"The World – A Divine Family", B.K. Narendra, India

Mahikari Youth Creation, Mahikari Youth Group, Belgium

The future will be a new lease on life, full of infantile purity, fresh air and kaleidoscopic hues and colours. The future is the dream of the children, the vision of the young and the prospect of the old. Meantime, it is a brand new canvas on which people apply their respective favourite colours to form the most beautiful images. The background of the future is golden and brilliant. This future is the Golden Age, which is known as Heaven or the Western Happy Pure Land by the Buddhists. Peace and beauty are what mankind yearn for. Dark colours will soon be replaced by the golden colours. A new era is moving slowly towards us.

Zhang Xiao Lei, Artist, China

I wish to see a world of spiritual joy, of solidarity, of harmony, where beauty is true beauty, where there is no selfishness, where someone else's well-being is my own, where the houses are white and full of flowers and where people enter them as if they were a temple, where people smile from their hearts.

Ana Ines Villareal, Pianist, Argentina

"Dynamic Faces of a Couple", Tobias Butama, Kenya

In a Better World:

Human Rights are respected and upheld and the dignity and integrity of all people is assured.

人权得到尊重和维护，人人的尊严和人格得到保障。

Права человека, достоинство и целостность человеческой личности гарантированы и защищены.

Les droits de la personne humaine sont respectés et préservés; la dignité et l'intégrité des personnes sont garanties.

تحترم حقوق الانسان وتؤيد، وتضمن سلامة وكرامة الناس جميعاً.

Se respetan y se defienden los derechos humanos y se garantizan la dignidad y la integridad de todas las personas.

2 HUMAN RIGHTS, DIGNITY & INTEGRITY

In our better world, the dignity and divinity of humanity inspire respect, altruistic interactions, benevolence and a compassionate attitude. Each person leads a life revealing the natural beauty of their innate God-given gifts. Their inner strength of truth, with a real balance of love and law, results in happiness in all relationships. The perfect person is a being of complete integrity with all talents and virtues.

B.K. Janki, Spiritual Leader, India

Life is a gift which each human being has the right to live without stepping on the rights of others.

Margarita Maria Ospinal, Colombia

My vision is of a society in which each person is seen as unique and precious.

Malcolm Pearce, Director, Australia

I see myself as a nice, clean and tidy boy who is helpful to lonely and hurt people.

David M. Joyce, Student, New Zealand

Individuals should have the right to determine their own destiny.

Tafilani Pomfret Machacha, Geologist, Botswana

Rebecca Alker-Jones, Age 12, Australia

Every being, of whatever origin, has blood and tears of the same colour, and therefore the respect and justice he deserves should be of the same dimension.

Oscar Adolfo Parody, Writer, Argentina

Major religions of the world would work together in a spirit of ecumenism where each respects the religious views of the other.

Sr. Augustino Tualasea, Religious Administrator, Western Samoa

Every individual should strive to concern himself with what is happening around him; stand up and speak up for others' rights; have his feelings, thoughts and home-grown wisdom be known and respected, if not appreciated. He should get involved and not be wrapped up in himself alone.

Charisse G. Novales, Business-Planning Assistant, United Arab Emirates

The source of human motivation is development of oneself. The basic condition of development is to seek truth, kindness and beauty. Development should be peaceful.

Wan-Jinn Wa, Scientist, Taiwan

Apply the same criteria when discussing the problems and the issues of humankind without discrimination with respect to colour, sex, religion or race.

Ali Mohammed Fahrow, Minister of Education, Bahrain

"Smile and Spread Happiness", Damian Knox, Australia

Let all peoples have equal rights and opportunities to pursue their legitimate national, economic, and cultural aspirations while protecting and respecting the rights of others.

Abdallah Y. Al Mouallimi, Chief Operating Officer, Saudi Arabia

My vision is of a world in which all are recognized as valuable, women and men, old and young, all races and colours, all life forms; a world where people are not defined by role, job, wealth, relationship, race, but by the dignity of their own being.

Jo Pacsoo, UK

We underline the word respect as we recognize the dignity and integrity of each human being; respect for human rights so that there may be social, political and economic justice, and brotherhood amongst humanity.

Joaquin Gantier Valda, Director, Casa de la Libertad, Bolivia

Every person would be leading their own destiny and would have the right to die with dignity.

Maria Santamaria, Medical Officer, Switzerland

My vision would be for a world without wars and discrimination, a world where all people are recognized as equal, where sportsmen and sportswomen can compete together in harmony.

Sir Garfield Sobers, Cricketer, Barbados

I see a world where the real value of man is fully recognized; that of human dignity, peace, self-respect and respect for others. I see a world where the urge to progress would not be to accumulate riches but rather to improve the human condition.

Roshni Bundhoo, Student, Mauritius

Cartoon for CAFAM's Youth contest on Human Rights,
John Alexander, Age 15, Colombia

Respect for whatever one's
faith, belief or religion.
Abdul Ghani Bujang,
Educator, Brunei Darussalam

Each of us should strive to
know and be himself,
And strive to accept others
for themselves,
Whether they know who
they are or not,
For you know who they are -
they are people just like you,
striving to know and be
themselves.
Abraham Barzeli,
Psychologist, Israel

I hope to establish a world
where "freedom" and
"security" coexist, where
"power" is limited by
"reason" and "rights" are
fully protected.
Yan Jiaqi, Professor, China

I think that there is a progression in the way human rights are fulfilled. I do not believe that we will be able to accomplish full implementation of the declarations and conventions unless we make sure that the basics are in place. When we talk about human rights you cannot forget the word choice - choice within your circumstances to do what you think is best and what you think is right because human rights go back to morality. It goes back to our basic understanding of self-worth and dignity. The true monitors of human rights are the people, those who are the victims and the beneficiaries. Even if a person is in dire circumstances because of being a refugee, a natural disaster victim, or a political prisoner, the individual is the monitor. Even if a person loses hope, that person still knows what is right and what is wrong. I believe that no matter how dire our situation is we have choice. When there is only one bite of food you have a choice to say let's split it or I give it to you because you are not well or I can decide to take it for myself. I may not have a choice as to whether I live in a tent if I am a refugee for example but my conscience gives me an understanding of what's right and what's wrong.

Marian B. Awwad, International Civil Servant, USA

Each child is an expression of love for this life. He comes to the world like a manifestation of the dignity, liberty and responsibility of his parents and becomes part of a society that has the resources to take care of him, feed him and permit his development through the values of compassion, love and non-violence.

Maria de la Luz Diaz,
Reiki Master, Chile

Global Cooperation at Kitano-cho Festival, Kobe, Japan (Beth Salisbury, Japan)

There would be more of a sense of responsibility towards children.

Nadim Suliman, Vice-Rector, Syria

I wish that the children would get a worthwhile wonderful life - that we shall not be divided into life sections - and that the seniors will rule and be treated with dignity and respect.

Karen Degett, Artist, Denmark

Children would have the right to receive care and protection, to the highest possible standard of health and educational facilities.

Erkan Rehber, Academic Staff, Turkey

Everyone is equal.
Everyone is happy.

Bryn and Eiry Spence, Students, Canada

There would be respect for and promotion of the right of peoples and nations to peace.

Ch. Purevdorj, Director-General,
The Mongolian People's Republic

Global Cooperation at Kitano-cho Festival, Kobe, Japan (Beth Salisbury, Japan)

Human values are to be directed towards upliftment of man's dignity and honour and not to the debasement of his position as entitled him by his being a human person.

What kind of world do we want? A world where peace reigns, where children do not die of starvation, where families reconcile among themselves, where God lives to strengthen people in their trials and problems ... this vision is a noble aspiration. This ideal gives an impetus to make it into reality.

Jaime L. Cardinal Sin, Archbishop of Manila, Philippines

For Maori people, our vision for the future is contained in the vision which our ancestors passed to us as a treasure, not to keep but to realize. This is why we have such special care and concern for our children and for the transmission to them of the wisdom and the warmth which we ourselves received. We are simply the vessels through which their vision becomes real. We shall protect the language in which that vision is encoded, and the land from which all sustenance comes. But most of all, we remember that we are the living memories for those who went before and wish for us everything that is good in the world.

Te Arikinui Dame Te Atairangikaahu - "Dame Te Ata", New Zealand

My vision of the future is of a world in which cultural differences are respected both within and between countries; where the worth and dignity of all human beings are acknowledged and placed at the centre of all thought and action; where true appreciation of each other's cultures will eliminate the impulse to dominate others.

Gloria Nikoi, Former Foreign Minister, Ghana

In many countries health problems stem from inefficient water distribution systems. The sewage and fresh water become mixed and then you have to teach the local population to boil water. What I have found, by experience, is that you cannot persuade people to do something that is going to make their life difficult, no matter how rational the reason. You may teach them how and when to boil the water, but they don't do it unless it is easy to do.

The question also arises as to what extent the government has a right to interfere with an individual. I have come to some practical conclusions. Let us say that there is a kind of vaccine which is very effective but also has some side effects. Do I have the right to give someone that vaccine? The answer will depend on who is going to be affected if I don't use the vaccine. If only the person getting the vaccine is in danger, then he or she has the right to refuse to take it. But if others are going to be endangered by the refusal, then the the right to refuse does not exist.

A. Mates, Director of Laboratories, Israel

Kirk Kolenberg, Belgium

"Choices" is a catchword, because to give to a person the right to choose what he or she wants or to say that giving choice is the aim for human development is a lovely perception but there's another side of the equation - you must have the possibility to choose also. For example when I was in a poor country driving through the villages I noticed children carrying water; not just children but also middle aged people and elderly people too - three generations carrying water. What choices do these kids have in life? Do they have any choice? Is it their desire to carry that water for all of their lives? This is the other part of the equation. To say human development is to have choice is lovely - to say it is one thing but you must also see whether the environment where you live can really allow the possibility of choice. So when we are looking for a better world, saying that this should be the ultimate goal, we are talking about the need for structures. If we are to say that there should be choice then it is the obligation of those who have power to create an environment that allows others to have such choices. That is why when I talk about human rights, the freedom from want is tremendously important.

Uner Kirdar, International Civil Servant, Turkey

Every human being would have the right to develop talent and to have work according to this talent, because it is necessary for individuals to live in happiness.

J. Nemec, Czech Republic

Much of the misery, war and misdevelopment that plagues our planet comes from our incapacity to see and hear one another, to grant humanity to those who are different. Without an effort by the more powerful and technologically advanced people at recognizing the validity, richness and active participation of the multiple adult voices from the zones and lands where most of the globe's inhabitants live, there will be no lasting peace. It is time that individuals, communities and countries proclaimed that the first breakfast on everybody's table each morning is more important than the third car in a few garages.

Ariel Dorfman, Writer, Chile

Every human being would believe in non-violence.

C. K. Gurung, Retired, Bhutan

Cartoon for CAFAM's Youth Cartoon Competition on the Rights of the Child, Colombia

In this search of a better world, the woman should not be kept aside. She needs to participate actively in this immense work. She needs to be listened to, as she hasn't been as yet. No better conception of the world is possible without the woman's participation. My suggestion: Make women meet so as to share their views about a better world.

Longo Tshuete, Zaire

We can see a better and valuable world without national antagonisms in which racial discrimination has been effaced according to the slogan: "all people are brothers" and where peace reigns above all. Every one of us is a particle of the big organism called community of the world.

Creative Group, Poland

Last summer, in cooperation with the Foundation for the Defence of Dignity of the Disabled, I succeeded in sending a Polish team to the Abilympics in Hong Kong. Abilympics stands for Ability Olympics for able-bodied and disabled persons. Over two thousand participants from eighty countries competed in skills such as computer programming, electronic product assembly, engineering, drawing, typing, lathe-turning, photography, silk screen printing, knotting, jewelry making, ceramics, and driving skills, just to mention a few. One of the Polish participants was a thirty-four year old poet, the author of a beautiful lyric "Do not be afraid to live". She has been confined to a wheelchair since her childhood, and living with her parents, spends most of the time at home; she has never travelled. Despite the discomfort caused by the heat and humidity in Hong Kong, despite some health problems she experienced while there, despite the linguistic, cultural and geographical barriers, upon her return to Poland and beaming with excitement she told me: "You have changed my life. This trip was the best experience I ever had. I feel accepted, I feel able, I found friends, I dare to live. In fact I feel like climbing the mountains!" she added. "I think you already did" - I replied.

Barbara Hansen, Honorary President, Poland

When every child, woman and man enjoy their dignity, integrity and human rights, then the world will enjoy the harmony and peace that we all need.

Leonor Gonzalez Mira, Singer/Actress, Colombia

Winner of 1st prize, Senior Section, in the Global Cooperation Art Contest "My Idea of a Better World," Hong Kong, Wong Nai Kei, Age 14, Hong Kong

In a Better World:

People live in ways that preserve nature's ecological balance in an environment that is beautiful and clean.

人们在自然生态平衡得到保护、优美清洁的环境中生活。

Человек живет в гармонии с природой, оберегает ее экологический баланс, красоту и чистоту.

Chacun vit de manière à préserver l'équilibre écologique de la nature dans un environnement agréable et non pollué.

يعيش الناس بأساليب تحفظ للطبيعة توازنها الحياتي الجميلة في بيئة نظيفة وجميلة .

Las personas viven de modo tal que se preserva el equilibrio ecológico de la naturaleza en un medio ambiente hermoso y limpio.

3 IN BALANCE WITH NATURE

I opened my eyes; beautiful day!
Blue skies so clear, so clear my mind inside.
The birds all around with such feeling
Start to sing lovely songs.
Now I step outside, out into the light.
Overflowing happiness, pouring out as from a spring.
The leaves on all the trees, blowing in the breeze,
Start to dance, all around rustling leaves.
Seems like something good is gonna happen
Wrapped in that good feeling all around.

Hiroyuki Minami, Musician, Japan

I would like nature in a better world to be a green nature (with green grasses) with lots of fresh water (lakes, rivers, seas, family swimming pools) lots of flower gardens and trees in which the birds fly. I would like a nature with a light wind in the trees to bring a fresh breeze. I would also like to see large and small animals in the parks and zoos.

Godelieve Uwimana, Student, Rwanda

There will be a time.... when the children of the earth will have respect and love for every flower and tree, every blade of grass, aye, for all the creatures seen and unseen that live on land and in the sea.

Rosie Emery, Musician, Canada

The ratio of our population to the world's resources is harmonious and the population is widely spread.

Roundtable Group, Switzerland

It would always be spring.
With my brush I brush out the entire world.
I chase away the bad weather.
I would have a big house,
With a wood by the side of my pretty house.
I would have rabbits to nibble my carrots.
I would have birds to peck at my grains.
I would have a river to hear the running water.
Wolves would explain to me their problems
And the owls would tell me their tales.

Creative Group, Students, France

People have the awareness that they are natural, organic beings, living in a natural organic world.

Barbara A. Chase, Librarian, Barbados

"Animal Life", Irvis Mann, Age 16, Trinidad & Tobago

A world where the natural forces will work perfectly in balance, thus giving the best climatic atmosphere.

George Marroudis, Clerk, Greece

Environmental protection must begin at home, for home is the place where values are shaped and nourished. If something is cherished, you take it home. It is at home that the individual is empowered to do whatever he can in terms of changes in behaviour and lifestyle.

Some fundamental lifestyle changes will have to be undertaken regarding the use of material resources. A few months ago, I was at a very prestigious hotel and in the bathroom there were two big bars of soap even though I was only staying one night. I asked myself why do I need so much soap as once you unwrap it it's gone. I pointed this out to the management who said they would try to get more individual sizes and also recycle old soap. However what was more interesting than what the hotel said was that I was uncomfortable in the presence of waste.

People are beginning to see that the marketplace is a place of values in transaction. You are not only trading things but you are also trading values. In making a purchase you are also making a statement, casting a vote. Businesspeople also have to rethink their values. "Do we induce and entice people to buy useless products, to overbuy unnecessarily so that we can keep our market going?"

Beginnings such as these can bring about a revolution in consciousness and values, with effects on a larger scale. I think there is a fundamental revolution taking place in values and that earth values are beginning to become much more manifest. In every genuine revolution the people usually get there first and I think if I were to put my money anywhere I'd put it on the people.

Noel Brown, International Civil Servant, Jamaica

"How fine to greet a morning washed by yesterday's rain", Joan M. Reynolds, USA

I feel that the awakening of the human conscience will come from traditions that already belong to people, when people are able to reidentify with traditions already available to them. Ethics have never been manufactured overnight. They cannot be prescribed like medicine - it's a question of civilization. Perennial traditions dictate that you should not cut a banyan tree because it is sacred or that you should not hunt a particular fish in a certain season - traditions such as these can create the necessay ethical framework. Any laws that try to act above and independently of the ethical traditions of the major religions of the world and of the indigenous peoples will make no difference.

Vandana Shiva, Physicist, India

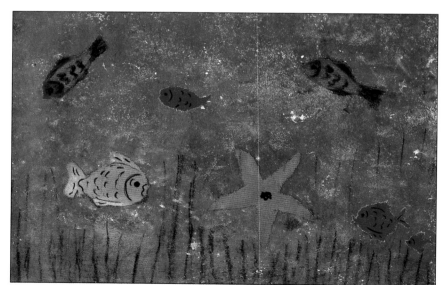

"Vorrei vivere nel mare", Giordano Caruso, Age 5, Italy

I was watching a star and it come and sit on the Earth near me and ask me to sit on her back. And then we left out of the world and I feel so happy and ask her where are you taking me? She said to CareALot world. She take me to such a big and very beautiful garden that I think that I'm in Paradise and I saw red flower in place and the yellow in place and the white in place. And in the bottom there was a gold flower and that flower means Greenland. Then we talk about Clean Land in her world and she give me good and simple way about clean, that there wasn't rubbish. Then I ask her to take me back to my home. The star told me that this world will be our world in the year 2000 and I hope from God that our world will be just like CareALot.

With my love,
Muna Falah Farhood, Student, Jordan

People in my country say that The Small World (the human personality) should live in harmony with the Big World (the surrounding society). All human beings can have peace only if they create harmony in their relationships with nature, society and the Divine Being.

Selo Soemardjan, Professor, Indonesia

A supremely glorified earth like a delightful heaven. Splendid cities and countrysides, with delightful roads having no dust, lined with flowers and trees, peopled with happy men and women, with children; good animals grazing on the green fields.

Mundinyi F. Ngombiga, Civil Engineer, Cameroon

Appropriate educational programmes at all levels of society world-wide will contribute to a vast decrease in the world population. This is crucial to all other visions and is the only way to eliminate poverty and stop such ecological disasters as the greenhouse effect and the destruction of the rainforests and with them the habitat for ever-dwindling plants and animals.

May Drake, Teacher, UK

There is balance in nature, fresh air and fresh water for everyone; utilization of sun, wind and water power, effective and efficient use of resources; responsible agriculture; organic architecture both in forms and materials; respect for all living things.

Creative Group, Iceland

We need to start to change our way of life, the food we eat, what we drink, how we sleep. Now we are existing in a technosphere, a man-made sphere which is interfering with the natural balance of nature. There is the growing awareness that we live in one world and if one part of the world suffers the whole world suffers. We want quality in our lives not just quantity.

Farkhonda Hassan, Geologist, Egypt

In our ideal world we foresee a world with pure air, seas and rivers, which are maintained by clean agriculture and industrial technology. The human population is distributed into villages, with life-styles that sustain ecological balance. There is rational usage of all natural resources. Energy would be ecologically pure and drawn from solar, wind and magnetic sources. All materials are recycled, production is free of waste and there is perfect agriculture based on natural fertilizers.

Roundtable Group, Ecologists, Russia

My vision of the world is one in which man has reached the point of understanding that he is not the owner of nature but forms a part of her. The balance between man and nature is essential to the possibility of life on this planet.

Emmanuel, Singer, Mexico

My personal vision is that the decade of the 90s will address the global issue of increased environmental degradation in both developing and

"The end of the night", Alfonso Machorro, Mexico

developed nations. I envisage greater environmental awareness to combat counter-productive consequences of deforestation, soil erosion, beach erosion, desertification, silted-up reservoirs, water pollution, solid waste pollution, pesticide resistant insects and loss of flora and fauna valuable species.

Manyu M. Kamara, Senator, Liberia

There should be a global commitment for the protection of environment for the welfare of the people, and commitment of the neighbouring state(s) to protect and preserve the natural environment.

Golam Rahman, Vice-Chancellor, Bangladesh

The world is at the crucial moment of having to decide before finishing the 20th century the conditions that will enable the survival not only of humanity but maybe of all existing life forms on earth.

Arquimedes Canese, Doctor, Paraguay

"Ice Bird", Manfred Scharpf, Germany

Blow O wind, blow!
Blow away our disillusions,
our despairs and unhappiness;
Sweep away the ties that bind us
to hatred, jealousy, greed, grief
and to the thirst of power and wealth;
Carry away our shattered dreams,
our bleak and immoral thoughts
to barren deserts where they
will not reach human folk.
When you come back,
please bring gusts of love
to pour in our hearts;
Bring hope, peace and serenity
to our wretched souls;
Bring us messages of brotherhood
from all over the world.
Blow O immortal wind and
fulfil these wishes of mortal souls.
We shall be grateful if you do.
Blow O wind, blow!

Mitra Thumiah, Clerk, Mauritius

Anon., Zaire

Anon., Zaire

We live in a world with clean air and water. Our cities are built in harmony with the environment and we have beautiful palaces for people to meet. We have the utmost regard for the natural processes and live in harmony with animals. We practise organic farming and strive to maintain the ecological balance. Waste is disposed of carefully and we use environmentally friendly sources of power.

Creative Group, Ireland

I would like a world with streets made of grass and flowers connecting all the roads of the earth, upon which one could walk barefoot, warmed by a pure sun, breathing clean air. A green world connected and united by the beauty of nature in its free state, born and grown spontaneously, that only dies to give new seeds and new life.

Antonella Talarico, Italy

Life on earth, such a marvellous combination of different forms, is in danger because the human race represents a menace to many species. Everyday the number of plant and animal species in danger of extinction increases. The planet is being changed in such a form that it becomes a good habitat for humans; we build cities, roads, parks, etc. which make human life easier and more enjoyable. We humans make use of natural resources often without any concern for our obligation to replace what we use. The problem is that by changing the form of nature we are destroying ecosystems necessary for animal and plant life which die with the change of environment.

Typical of tropical forests is the immense variety of species. Attention is drawn by those magnificent great trees, which arouse the imagination of many. But do people stop to think what a forest really is? Aren't orchids hanging from the branches of the trees also an integral part of the forest? And the animals? Certainly deer and armadilloes also belong to the jungle. If we really think it over, insects, frogs, birds and little rodents are equally part of the forest as are trees, climbing plants and lichens.

Humanity has found benefit in the use of many natural resources; from the trees, wood is gained; animals can be used for food and furs; flowers provide ornament; there are so many reasons to cut and kill some living part of the jungle. But by removing any part of the forest, the habitat necessary for the survival of some species changes. Humanity has so many individuals, that we have to create the consciousness

"A World for All", Loreto Convent Primary School, Kenya

that if industry keeps on removing resources from the forest these will shortly disappear. The forest is a complex ecosystem which allows life to each and all creatures living in it. Systematic removal of any one part will endanger the rest. Interdependence of the enormous variety of animals and plants is so complex that even if we plant all of the species which occur in nature, we still would not have a jungle. Plants and animals need to be of different ages; young animals often need the presence of adult plants for their survival and vice versa. Therefore reforestation (to create a jungle) is an impossible task. Conservation is of utmost importance.

Werner Steinvorth, Orthopaedic Surgeon, Costa Rica

My hope for the 1990s is that they will lay the basis for a millenium in which humankind shows that it has learnt its greatest lesson - that if we are to survive and realize our potential, we must extend the circle of our compassion to all living creatures, regardless of colour, creed, race or species. We are all kin, sharing the same needs, joys, and right to liberty and life. If we persist in believing that we can outsmart Nature and forever exploit the environment for our own selfish ends, 'She' will have the last laugh, and the Earth will be at peace - without us.

Jon Wynne-Tyson, Author, UK

I should not bother the bees,
I should not damage God's lovely trees.
Wild flowers should be left alone,
Nor should I write upon a stone.
All nature is a wonderful treasure,
God made it for his people's pleasure.

Luyla Segal, Age 11, Canada

There's a trend in Western societies towards a cleaner environment but this involves a deep contradiction in having to pay a high price for a clean environment; for example not using a car but public transportation and not changing one's way of life. The mentality still is to enjoy the privilege of the private car and consumption without restraint. The forthcoming years should be interesting because most western societies have been based on industrial production which it was thought would always grow, and which was essentially geared towards armament in one way or another. Now if we start reducing the production of armaments, given the importance of that industry in the western world, I don't really know where we are going. I think we are going to be in a recession for quite a while before we find alternative ways of employing all this production capacity that will become idle. We cannot just close all the factories and wait. So this trend towards reduction of armaments is very interesting, very gratifying, but might cause some heavy economic consequences and be the beginning of the "remise en cause" of the whole western society.

Christian Rolling, Interpreter, France

"Heaven", Margaret R. Goodenough, UK

Cartoon which appeared in "A Tarde", a Brazilian newspaper, Paulo Serra, Brazil

My vision is of large human settlements that are neither urban nor rural, but ecologically in balance with their bio-regions and the ecology of the planet. These "ecopolis" will be "nutritionally self-reliant human settlements." Such settlements solve the problems of ecological degradation and hunger at the source.

Jac Smit, Futurist, USA

My own vision of the future is one in which the children grow up as fully rounded individuals partly through learning about and living out what it is that links each one of us to the earth. To make peace with the earth, we must experience it directly, as mud between toes, as the flash of a butterfly's wing, as the surge of new life every spring. The education of each and every child should be underpinned by this kind of earth wisdom.

Jonathon Porritt, Environmentalist, UK

My vision for a better world is one in which the human race rises above its petty greed and selfishness and decides to integrate its collective wisdom and intelligence to save the ecosphere and the creation. If we can develop the mechanisms to destroy the earth, we can also save it.

Helen Caldicott, Physician, Australia

"Mutual Respect, Mutual Assistance",
G. Dyemchenko, Russia

One day I was walking in my new world. I saw a lot of birds, beautiful birds. I looked and looked but I saw nothing like a paper on the streets and paths. I looked at myself. How clean I was. I saw the people behaving; I started to smile at them. I looked at the companies, they had good and beautiful cars. I looked everywhere. I saw no accidents no thieves. I like my world as it is I say. I looked at all the shops. I saw they had cheap things. I went to the heroes' fighting field; there was a sign written: No more wars. I like my world as it is I say.

George Sibotshiwe, Student, Age 10, Zimbabwe

We live in a clean environment where we do not dominate nature but we coexist with nature. We live in beautiful houses built of perfumed sandalwood. The buildings are designed in such a way as to reflect sunlight and allow free circulation of fresh air. There are no doors and windows since permanent security prevails in our community. We use electricity generated from sunlight and we are thus assured of an all-renewable energy system.

Roundtable Group, Mauritius

Trash lined streets are only one indication of the crisis confronting our neighbourhoods, the nation, and the world. Reluctantly, we have accepted that styrofoam serves up equal parts of refreshment and environmental ruin. We have begun to suspect that the boxes, wrappings and trimmings of our beloved holiday season are responsible for an unequalled production of litter and refuse. Finally, we have begun to think about the popular conveniences that will ultimately inconvenience our existence.

"Biodegradable", the rallying cry of the seventies, should have had an impact on our fanatical use of plastic

"Let's Live in a Healthy and Pleasant Environment", Narain Kawsar, Age 12, Mauritius

bags and superfluous packaging, but it didn't. We stored that knowledge away in styrofoam packing filler and continued to be silent and inactive about our responsibility to manage our modern miracles. Responsibility is the key to recycling. As newspapers pile up in our homes, we think about who is responsible for bundling them up and carting them off for recycling. We think about who is responsible for the milk shake carton that just missed the garbage, or the extra shopping bags we request. We think, and ultimately decide, that it is someone else's job - the sanitation department, the manufacturers, the fast food vendors. Actually, each of us is responsible because recycling benefits each of us in important, lasting ways.

Responsibility for recycling also relates to how we dispose of unwanted possessions such as furniture and clothing. Industry has the same problem that individuals have because they must decide how to dispose of unwanted by-products. Solutions must represent a collaboration between individuals and industry based on a shared responsibility. Some creative people have grappled with this problem and come up with some innovative strategies to protect the environment and benefit humankind.

Sharon M. Cadiz, Educator, USA

My vision is inspired by the philosophy of our indigenous people: there is no sense in having reverence for life without having reverence for the one who made it possible for us to live in a healthy body, and in balance with other forms of life such as the planet, the rivers, the trees and the animals. I'd like to see reverence for the Great Creator.

Marcos Terena, Indigenous Leader, Brazil

Warawut Buathong, Thailand

In a Better World:

The planet's natural and abundant resources are shared equitably and the basic human needs of all people are provided for.

公平地分享地球上丰富的自然资源，保证人人的基本需要。

Щедрые природные богатства планеты распределяются справедливо и основные потребности человека находят удовлетворение.

Les ressources naturelles abondantes de la planète sont équitablement partagées, et les besoins essentiels de chacun sont assurés.

تتم المشاركة في مصادر الطبيعية الوافرة بالتساوي، وتؤمن حاجات جميع الناس الأساسية.

Los recursos naturales y abundantes del planeta se comparten de manera equitativa, y se provee a las necesidades humanas basicas de todas las personas.

4 NEEDS BASIC TO LIFE

There must be respect for human life. Let the human being be healthy and fulfilled. There must be enough food, clothing and shelter for everyone.

Ahmad El Wafee, Mauritania

My vision is that all the world's people would have a roof over their head, food on the table, and nourishment for the soul as well. I also wish for the same love and respect we share with each other to be shown to all animal and plant life on the planet.

Olivia Newton John, Singer/Actress, Australia

I would like to see a world where joy was an everyday expression. This would mean that no human being ever died of hunger, cold or lack of medical attention. It need not be a world where each person was rich, indeed my world would have totally different values than the world of today. It would be a world where all accepted responsibility and learned to share their lives, energies and gifts, yet without making martyrs of themselves; a world where people learned to be good not only to others but to themselves.

Kathleen Stansfield, Adult Educator, UK

We would like to make a world where there is a magic drink that gives us nature's own qualities.

Creative Group, Students, Denmark

All of us in the neighbourhood have enough food to eat - in fact we are sharing food with one another in overflowing platters and bowls. Everyone has a gainful employment; we can buy all our needs.

Flor B. Malicay,
Executive Director, Girl Scouts, Philippines

My better world is the paradise that God promised. In this paradise the old will be young, there will be enough food for everyone to eat. Nobody will fall sick but everyone will recover from any sickness they have.

Christine Mutefula, Student, Age 13, Mozambique

General health facilities are available for every human being.

Hesham Hassan Tawfiq, Tunisia

I wake up to the sound of birds singing in harmony and look out of my bedroom window to the sight of lush green fields in the distance partly sheltered from the warm sun by a few thickly leafed trees swaying gently in the wind. While dressing, I yawn, filling my lungs with pure, fresh air. I go to breakfast to see my family already seated and ready to eat all they want from their piled high plates.

I walk down the clean streets on my way to school. Everyone is smiling and greeting everyone they pass. At school there are no groups, everyone is as one.

"Oh no! I left my lunch at home!" No sooner are the words out of my mouth than "Don't worry, I'll give you some of mine. I have more than enough." "Thank you, my name is Kevin. What's yours?"

The day is coming to an end and as I walk home I think of how wonderful the day has been, but I am not sad that it is over as I know that I will sleep well tonight and that tomorrow the world will still be here, better than before!

Kevin Leliard, Student, Zimbabwe

Every human being would have equal access to health facilities to keep him healthy and content in spirit, mind and body.

A. Sattar Sikander, Dean, Pakistan

"Peace, Love, Harmony", Vinod K. Patel, Age 11, Kenya

"The Good Earth", Pupils of Hedehusene School, Denmark

In the health service of the immediate future every effort is made for the prevention of disease and the maintenance of high levels of hygiene.

Roundtable Group, Health Practitioners, Russia

Specialized treatment is available everywhere in the country including isolated places. The medical staff are not only trustworthy and professional but are humanitarian and compassionate in their attitude. They are ready to enlighten one on health education so that good habits can be instilled among the common people.

Creative Group, Malaysia

In the better world greater care and wisdom will be employed in ensuring a totally healthy start in life for the young human being. A woman preparing herself for motherhood, even before conception, would be surrounded by beautiful and uplifting influences.

H. M. Collymore, Orthopaedic Surgeon,
Trinidad & Tobago

"The Offering",
Ribeiro Farinha, Portugal

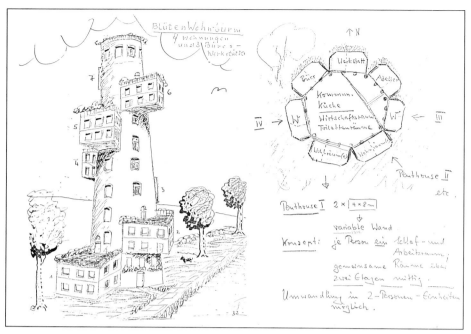

New architecture for the future could possibly look like this: community towers designed in the shape of a flower-bud to provide aesthetic appeal, conserve space and integrate all aspects of human life into a harmonious whole. Penthouse I provides each person with their own bedroom and workroom, with a central space on two floors, for communal sharing of a kitchen, bathroom and household workroom. Each penthouse is convertible into a two person unit.
Roundtable Group, Architects, Germany

All governments should cut down considerably on defence spending and divert more funds to food production, shelter for all and other basic human needs.

Emmanuel B. W. Campbell,
National Secretary, Sierra Leone

The natural resources of the earth must be protected for the benefit of present and future generations. This should be realized through careful planning and management.

Mithat Ozsan, Professor, Turkey

Power should be distributed to the extent of giving every urban and rural community the capacity to satisfy their own food needs and recycle their own wastes. Our lifestyle should not be in conflict with natural laws.

Ricardo A. Navarro, Technology Planner,
El Salvador

Anna Bettega, Age 6, Italy

All human beings would have adequate housing, healthy food, sewerage, potable water and sufficient remuneration from their work to provide for their own and their dependents' material necessities.

Luiz Pinguelli Rosa, Physicist, Brazil

While fostering a close community spirit, the housing policy will allow for individuality. Persons who prefer large homes on extensive grounds will have scope to satisfy these needs. Some people like apartment living, or a friendly chat with the neighbour over the fence, while others prefer more privacy. Whatever is one's preference in housing, society will seek to accommodate this as it is this individuality which will develop and enrich the nation.

Roundtable Group, Jamaica

There would be economic and political humanitarian cooperation between the north and the south, the richer and the poorer, so every human being would have shelter, food and water.

Alharith A. H. Hassan, Neuropsychiatrist, Iraq

Helping poor countries should be to solve the real problems rather than just sending help at crises, e.g. the initiation and foundation of agricultural schemes to solve food problems is better than sending food to these countries.

Faysal T. Abushama, Professor, Sudan

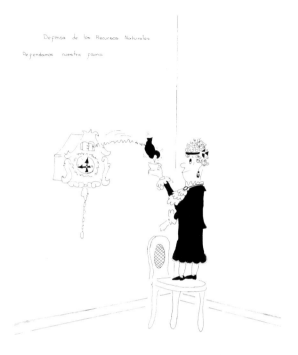

Cartoon for CAFAM's Youth contest on the Protection of Natural Resources, Jaime Campos Bernal, Colombia

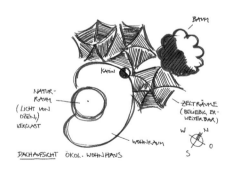

Global Cooperation Architecture – drawings prepared during a workshop with Architects in Austria

With careful planning from governments, develop community programmes (rural and urban) with representation of communities, directed to improve nutrition and health and taking advantage of renovated natural resources.

Ramiro Cruz, Physician, Nicaragua

Our obvious ability to feed the entire world would come to fruition if the incredible amount of time, energy and money now devoted to creating war machines might instead be concentrated on elevating the quality of life.

Jack Lemmon, Actor, USA

The survival of our planet requires of us a joint management which would benefit all of society. We must contemplate a change in our civilization to be defined as follows:

Establish a true division of labour and of the wealth produced as part of a redirection of the economy and of its environmental imperatives. This means providing for all, from cradle to grave, a citizen's income in exchange for social service.

The mistake is believing that the market economy will go on indefinitely; hence the reason behind the necessary redirection of the economy and a change in our civilization as a prerequisite for the survival of our planet.

Rene Jallifier-Verne, Retired, France

"Basic Human Needs", Nutaila Busaidy, Kenya

我们交出愛心，
做出更美好的明天

"Let's Give Our Heartfelt Love in Order to Have a Much Better Tomorrow", – winner of 2nd prize, Junior Section, in the Global Cooperation Art Contest "My Idea of a Better World", Hong Kong, Miss Chong Wing Min, Hong Kong

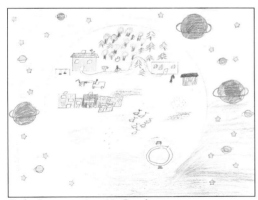

Erika Jansson, Age 11, Sweden

I would like that people treat their heart very well so that they can live longer and better.

Student, Escola Arrel, Spain

We must channel our energies towards building our physical selves by eliminating all harmful drugs and maintaining a well-balanced diet combined with a carefully developed exercise programme. This way our healthy body will reflect our happy mind and peaceful spirit.

Sally Yeh, Hong Kong

Each and every human being will have access to medical care and facilities necessary for his health and his physical, mental and spiritual well-being.

Ayite Manko d'Almeida, Dean, Togo

Ibrahim
Brian
Thompson,
UK

In a Better World:

All people have equal opportunities to realize their potential through an educational process that has human, moral and spiritual values at its heart.

通过以人道、道德、精神价值为核心的教育过程达到人人
都有平等的机会来实现自己的潜力。

Все люди имеют равные возможности для раскрытия своего потенциала через процесс обучения, стержень которого образуют гуманистические идеалы, нормы морали, духовные ценности.

Chacun a les mêmes chances de réaliser son potentiel grâce à un système d'éducation pénétré de valeurs humaines, morales et spirituelles.

للناس جميعا· الفرص المتساوية لتحقيق طاقاتهم بواسطة تربية
وتعليم تحمل القيم الانسانية والاخلاقية والروحية في قلبها .

Todas las personas gozan de igualdad de oportunidades para realizar su potencial por medio de un proceso educativo centrado en valores humanos, morales y espirituales.

5 EDUCATING MIND & SPIRIT

My vision is of an integral education, which is available to all equally and cultivates and develops the moral aspects of the individual.

Jose Hector Baseti Piriz,
Municipal Employee, Uruguay

Education starts in the family in such a way that each child is eager to learn. Schools are part of our society and are financed by the state to ensure equality of standards. Children learn to read and write and study literature, maths, art, music, astronomy, astrology and psychology.

There is an emphasis on culture and ecology and a sense of fantasy is developed. Sports are played on each of the school days. Teachers are well paid, specialized and able to sense pupils' needs. They use different educational methods according to pupils' varying abilities. Teachers are patient, tolerant, kind, cultured, self-confident and fair and have an interest in and good knowledge of the subjects they teach.

Roundtable Group, Educators, Russia

The school is seen as a mini-community and so cooperative principles are encouraged. It is a safe and inviting place for children to be. Teachers are mindful of the potential of each child but without expectations. The education structure allows for consultation and cooperation between parents and the school. There is respect between teachers and children. Education allows the development of self-respect and so respect for society and for the environment.

Roundtable Group,
Health Professionals, UK

"Education is a Rainbow to a Brighter World",
Ophelia Arp, Age 10, Micronesia

Education in our better world is more value-oriented. Emphasis is laid on the three 'H's - Head, Heart and Hands rather than on the three 'R's (Reading, WRiting and ARithmetic).

Roundtable Group, Mauritius

Educational opportunities should be offered freely to all citizens of the world, no matter who or where they are.

Steven Edmund Winduo, Lecturer, Papua New Guinea

The better school is surrounded by a landscape in which the pupils themselves have planted trees and flowers. Everyone sees the school in the way he would like it to be. In the classrooms the walls are painted in one colour - mostly a soft celestial blue. The pictures hanging on the walls show photos from other countries. There is always something in the pictures that fills one with a sense of well-being. The tone of voice of the children and teachers is full of harmony. No one thinks or says anything unpleasant or destructive. In the classroom there is a tree growing out of the floor. This tree is a copper beech. And anyone looking at it sees how much oxygen it gives to people every day.

Creative Group, Students, Austria

I am deeply concerned about the quality of the education which our young people receive. They should be encouraged to look beyond their immediate gratification. Educators must also begin to help them sense the needs and expectations of their own society. This kind of training complements the wisdom gained during the educational process and allows the adults of tomorrow to make sound decisions which will carry them towards a desirable future.

Abdol Ali Gharaati, Dean, Iran

In our world the education system is one which seeks to bring out the characteristics and talents, potentials and specialities within the individual. There is no set time-period for the completion of the education process, rather, it is a continuous, lifelong series of experiences. Each one learns or discovers at his or her own pace and according to his personal desire and interests. Education is a celebration of life.

Barbara Anne King and Carole Bridge,
Educators, Jamaica

The formation of young leaders with integrity, bravery and with a deep sense of justice.

Marisa de los Andes,
Teacher, Ecuador

The students have the right to choose the school, the subjects and the system of education.

Roundtable Group, Bulgaria

Reckem, Brazil

Costa Rican Schoolchildren
Creating Their Vision of a
Better World.
(Diane Tillman, USA)

Please, Mr., Mrs., and Miss Educators, consider yourselves as educators and not as the slaves of one science or the other, be it history or chemistry, philology or electronics.

You have to select your subject matter carefully in view of the needs of those who as grown-ups are going to live through the end of the twentieth and into the first half of the twenty-first century. What you must bear in mind is that not only do we have to prepare future administrators, economic and other leaders but that in the first place we have to prepare better human beings, equipped with spiritual values. The task is not easy but education never is and it is not a question of possibility but of necessity. It is not easy but it is necessary to incorporate an equilibrium between personal, local, national, regional, and international values.

You will have to explain the place, the responsibility and the possibilities of individuals and social groups in the world of today and the expectations they have for the world of tomorrow. You will draw attention to the great achievements some of us are enjoying and to the great problems we are facing. Thereby you will avoid diffusing too much pessimism or too much optimism.

You will make your pupils aware of the fact that cultural diversity is a richness for mankind and that the meeting and inter-penetration of cultures is perhaps an even greater wealth. You will consider human rights as the leitmotif of your educational impact. You will expose the perfidy of racism and racial discrimination. You will point out the necessity of a righteous social and economic world order. You will recognize the right to development, you will condemn the unbearable existence of poverty, sickness, illiteracy, famine and malnutrition. You will explain that man has become engaged in a struggle for supremacy with the technological apparatus he, himself has created in a struggle for survival in an environment which he, himself has deteriorated. You will stress wonderful things that have been achieved in the field of international understanding and cooperation.

You, educationalists, will examine these and other problems with your pupils and together you will come to concrete and progressive conclusions.

Paul Morren, Belgium

The challenge to education is clear. It is a challenge because it represents teaching values and changing and building up attitudes. Bringing the attention of children and adults alike to issues on peace and human rights is essential for a better future. It challenges one and all to stop and think, to reflect, to question. If teachers seriously want to take up the challenge of peace they need to begin personally to face value questions, and then to introduce them in the classroom.

In short, then, education for peace means inculcating in people an attitude - not only to the world as it is but as it can be. As educators we should not allow education to be asked to intervene, to make dramatic changes, to answer for so-called "failures" in the epilogue. The effects of education need to be at the beginning - in the first chapter. A coherent and powerful system of education may transform the future, perhaps even the immediate future, but we must not expect or allow others to expect that it can abruptly change the nature of the present. One thing is clear, education must bring about a mental renaissance, it must provide the stimulus to find and develop better ways of organizing a society which believes and accepts diversity and develops on trust.

A practical and applied education is about values. Education is life, providing us with a philosophy of living. The basic aim of education is that of helping the person think things out. Education is about change, growth and choice. It is there to help in the development of the individual, to help her/him make choices, to grapple with personal and social problems. Education is participation and application. It is about listening. Education is considerate, sympathetic, all-embracing, lifelong.

However, what does the word education truly mean? From amongst the many definitions, one which I believe and strongly adhere to emerges from the writings of Socrates. Socrates believed that all true education was self-education, one which aims at helping each individual to find herself/himself, that being the heart of the developing and learning process.

Christopher Bezzina, Principal, Malta

Any system of education must produce men and women ready to discern between right and wrong, to perceive and accept responsibilities and to order their conduct accordingly.

H. Rwantabagu, Professor, Burundi

Non-formal education must be accomplished strongly in every sector of the country. This is the appropriate way to liberty and democracy.

Sangcheol Kang, Professor, Republic of Korea

Education for all the world's children in communication skills emphasizing: respect of self and others, understanding, win-win philosophy, cooperative goal setting and trust of self and others.

Ruthann Pippenger, Peace Educator, Norway

"Operation Cooperation", a tandem tour of Tasmania, visited 16 schools and held creative groups at each, using the tandem as a symbol of cooperation. (Tom Ratcliffe, Australia)

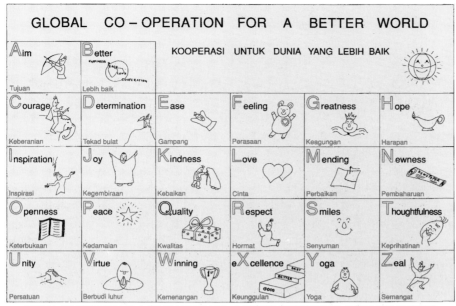

GLOBAL COOPERATION IS A PEACE MESSENGER INITIATIVE DEDICATED TO THE UNITED NATIONS

I grew up in a selective system of education. This system allowed and encouraged a few to succeed at the expense of the many who, by definition, had to fail. When I was young my self-esteem counted for nothing. It was as if my examination results were the only indicator of any account. But worse than that, those examination results seemed by some perverse morality to be translated into a measure of human worth. But those poor standards won't do for the education service any longer. Education was about competition then. Now, more than anything else, it should be about cooperation.

Over the last two or three decades the profession has been moving towards an education system which provides opportunities for all, but better than that enables young people to take advantage of those opportunities and even better than that enables children to feel worthy of those opportunities.

We are developing a system which recognizes and values the efforts of all. A system which provides opportunities for all children to experience success and to feel good about themselves. We now understand what a powerful motivating force success is and we are determined to provide an education system which brings that success into the lives of all our children.

John Berridge,
Senior Assistant Director,
(Education), UK

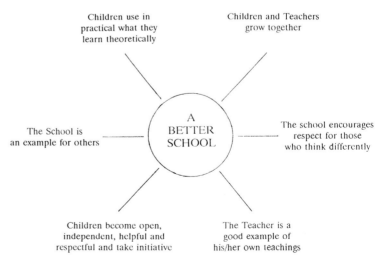

Children use in
practical what they
learn theoretically

Children and Teachers
grow together

The School is
an example for others

A BETTER SCHOOL

The school encourages
respect for those
who think differently

Children become open,
independent, helpful and
respectful and take initiative

The Teacher is a
good example of
his/her own teachings

Creative Group, Sweden

"Visualising a Better World", S. Munegalaung, Mauritius

I can make my class better by listening.
I can make my class better by combing my hair.
I can make my class better by being kind.
I can make my class better by tucking in my shirt.
I can make my classroom better by sweeping.
I can make my classroom better by dusting the shelf.

Barnabas Mukarakate, Age 9, Zimbabwe

Instruction must also make children and adolescents conscious of the multiple possible consequences of each individual behaviour for each and all the individuals in his environment and for himself. Every act has multiple consequences. Instruction should highlight that some behavioural patterns - positive, constructive, pro-social - lead to the well-being of the individual and those around him, while others lead to the opposite.

Rogelio Diaz-Guerrero, Professsor Emeritus, Mexico

There should be complete education for every kind of people so that they can understand the value of human life and their duties in the world.

Jayant Parmar, Student, India

Histories of people differ and therefore necessitate educational methods and subject matter that must be relevant and meaningful to these people of different origins.

Jacqueline Odle, Massage Therapist, Barbados

Schools have to know how to make the outside world the laboratory for learning and not think that everything can be learned inside the walls of the school.

Shlomo Sharan, Professor, Israel

My vision is of respect for the cosmic timing and rhythm in the growth of each individual.

Irene zur Lippe-Biesterfeld, Netherlands

A study of human behaviour should aim at understanding our place in the universe.

Beatrice H. Sandelowsky, Anthropologist, Namibia

Education is integral and seeks the global evolution of humanity on all levels, spiritual, mental, moral and physical, through a balance of values within all disciplines.

Konde Mbaku, Agricultual Cooperator, Zaire

Before heading for school I gave my Mum and Dad a kiss and they told me to have a good day. Today we have the subject 'Feelings'. We will learn about anger and how one controls it. Last week we talked about how happiness arises. The lesson begins in the morning and ends whenever we like. In Geography we learn about what is cultivated in different parts of the world. In Behaviour we learn how to behave towards others and towards ourselves. We also learn about cooperation and unity, and how to express our opinions. In Biology we learn about animals, plants and nature, and how we can continue to preserve it. In Language we learn to write the common language of the world. In Mathematics we learn how to calculate. In all the subjects we learn about things we can use later on in life. In our society there is a lot of computer science, so we learn about that. Pupils are often out visiting various working places.

When I came back home there was a message for me to 'phone Aunty Eileen from the opposite part of the globe. She told me that her community had just held an election, and that a woman had won it. Aunty had 'phoned her and congratulated her. We think it is very important to take part in everything that happens, you see. In the evening, I had a cozy time with my Mum and Dad.

Peter Andersen, Pupil, Age 11, Denmark

All people would be encouraged to develop their fullest potential keeping in mind to maintain a universal consciousness e.g. on one hand people are feeling good about themselves and what they are accomplishing in life and on the other hand, the encouragement to put back into a system that fosters this growth. Then there would never be a short supply of anything.

Gabriella Paoluzzi, Secretary, Canada

In the university of the future an inter-disciplinary approach will be the constant ideal to achieve efficient collaboration between the different sciences in such a way that a collective capacity to resolve problems and perceive success is increased. A multi-disciplinary approach involves a meeting of specialized areas within a determined context. Each will know the problematiques that the others are working on, will comment on their results and aims and will collaborate amongst themselves offering resources, contacts, knowledge and even advice.

Antonio Paoli, Professor, Mexico

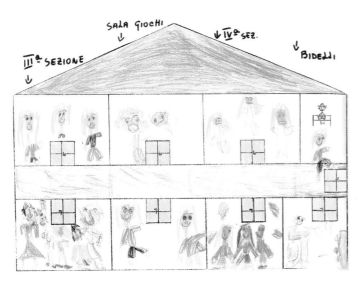

If you want to be cool go to school.

Enrique Eduardo, Age 5, USA

"This is My School", a painting painted for a primary school project "From the Real to the Fantastic – A journey to the World of Imagination", dedicated to Global Cooperation,
Soriano Nel Cimino School, Italy

"The Family", Ivo Calderon, Peru

In a Better World:

Life within the immediate family is loving, caring and fulfilling and is the foundation for harmony within the broader human family.

至亲家庭的生活充满着爱心、关怀和满足，并且是人类大
家庭和睦的基础。

В семье царят любовь, забота и мир, что создает основу для гармоничных отношений в семье человеческой.

La vie au sein de la famille proche est empreinte d'amour, de tendresse et chacun s'y épanouit; elle constitue le fondement de l'harmonie dans le cadre plus vaste de la famille humaine.

تكون الحياة فمن الأسرة المباشرة محبة ومراعية ومنجزة ، وهي أساس الحوافق فمن الأسرة الإنسانية الأوسع .

La vida dentro del núcleo familiar es afectuosa, solicita y satisfactoria y es el fundamento de la armonia dentro de la gran familia humana.

6 FAMILY: THE WORLD'S WARM CORE

My family makes my nation makes my world.
Roundtable Group, Singapore

Fetching water for mother
Giving milk to sister
Washing dishes on Sundays
This is cooperating at home
Let's cooperate in the house
And in the world.
Maiana Blum, Age 9, Brazil

Respect for human life and the desires of the individual to create only the children they really want and can care for should become a priority as it is vital for a better world. Spacing the family and every child a wanted child should be the aim.

Susan Hampshire, Actress and Author, UK

If each individual family unit plays its part in loving, caring and enriching the personalities, then the world can some day work as one big family.

Ryan Phillips, Prison Officer, Barbados

Doves as white as clouds sail in a sky.
The world is a beautiful garden full of
different coloured flowers.
The sun is bathing that land with golden rays,
adding more brightness to it.
People are like one big family;
a family in which everyone is equal, in which
divisions between rich and poor black and
white do not exist.
A family is like a spiritual community;
A community which does not accept either
language or national barriers;
where hands are joined in friendly embrace.
Love, truth and peace are reflected in the mirror of
human hearts and minds.
Katarzyna Sidoruk, Student, Poland

Old people will not have to live in loneliness, but due to their wisdom they will attain great regard from their families and live amongst them.
Guenther Radlherr, Guitarist, Austria

"The World – Our Home", Katarzyna Sidoruk, Poland

Design for a Christmas Card, Marcela Aller, Age 9, Argentina

"My Family", Huda Fahem Saleh, Age 16, Jordan

As a professional, a mother, and the wife of a dedicated national political figure working hard for social, moral and cultural upliftment, more self reliance and national economic independence, I am very sensitive to the issues meant to foster the status of the family in our society.

Women are a silent but strong force of love and compassion that can generate the mechanism of cooperation and harmony by our intentions and attitudes to foster goodwill and understanding for a better world.

If we can create good things in industries, make the island blossom to produce better fruits in agriculture, make good leaders of human destiny, we can certainly make the world better and more congenial for all of us to live in by making a symbiosis of all our qualities.

Lady Sarojini Jugnauth, First Lady of Mauritius

I awoke this morning with a refreshed inner clarity as I turned to face the soft luminosity flowing from my children's faces before me. We sat together and set forth our daily vision: starting with our personal lives, our community and then we visualized peace, light and love flowing through the earth and humanity. We shared our vision with gratitude and joy, knowing that every family, everywhere was sharing their vision today, in a lovingly unique way.

Laurie McFall, Teacher and Animator, Canada

Last week, I was reading a story on my radio show about a man who was asked by his son "Father, how much do you earn?" The man replied "800 pesos an hour". The kid asked "could you lend me 400 pesos?" but the father said no. Later, the father felt guilty and went to the child's room and said "here are the 400 pesos that you asked me for." The kid took the money and, reaching for 400 pesos from under his pillow, said "now I have 800 pesos so I can buy one hour of your time. Will you sell me one hour of your time?" The father could not believe that his son should have to ask to buy an hour of his time and he felt guilty.

A friend of mine heard the story on his way to work. That same day was his son's birthday and, before leaving home, his son had asked him if he would be back early to celebrate his birthday. He had told his son "I don't know - I have a conference this evening." But as soon as he arrived at the office he rearranged his schedule and went home early to celebrate his son's birthday. He felt that if he didn't make time for his family when they needed him then tomorrow might just be too late.

Malin Falu, Radio Host, Puerto Rico

Family life will offer affection and satisfaction and will contribute to the sense of a Universal Family that lives in harmony.

Jose Vanegas Covena, Industrial Chemist, Ecuador

MUTUAL LOVE: Because we feel that we belong to a family - the big family of the world - it is only proper that members of the same family should love each other, both in times of sorrow and happiness.

MUTUAL COMPASSION: As members of the big family of the world we are certainly unhappy to see the sufferings of others. Because we have mutual compassion, we want to see all members of the family enjoy a peaceful, happy and tranquil life.

MUTUAL RESPECT: Since we have the same position and responsibility in our family, we should ideally respect each other.

MUTUAL TRUST: In order to carry out our tasks and bear our respective responsibilities as well as possible in a quiet, harmonious, agreeable, balanced and wise manner, we must have mutual trust.

MUTUAL HELP: Well aware that members of the family do not have the same potentials and abilities in every field, we should therefore help each other.

MUTUAL COMPLEMENTARITY: Since within a family we need and depend upon each other - whether as a government official, businessman, farmer, fisherman etc. - it would be ideal if we were complementing each other.

MUTUAL ABSTENTION FROM INTERFERENCE:
Obviously the big family of the world consists of different

"Living together as one", Lailah Adnan, Age 11, Kenya

families of nations, and of small families inhabiting all parts of the world, having different backgrounds, customs and traditions, religions, art and culture etc. We must, as a consequence, seriously consider abstaining from interfering in the internal affairs of others, unless requested to do so.

Madame Tien Soeharto, First Lady of Indonesia

I sat under a tree which had merged branches and lots of leaves. My mind went away from this land of problems, wicked people and pollution. I closed my eyes. I felt my soul climbing slowly, slowly. A small cloud carried me into the wide horizon. I could see a lot of clouds and stars until I came to a foreign land which I hadn't seen before. The smell was marvellous and the singing of the birds was like that of those at home. It was a land of love, happiness, satisfaction and purity - a green land with lovely gardens and fruits. It is a paradise. There are kind hearted people in this land who received me with a warm welcome. The head of the family, the father, took his children into the garden to plant trees.

I saw the young help the older and the older love the young. The families were all working together with a strong will to grow trees. I wished I was one of them. After a while they all went home. Mothers were cooking. Children helped their mothers and husbands picked fruits. Their eyes shone with the hope of the future. We sat at the table to eat but we didn't start until they had fed some of the poor and unfortunate. I was extremely happy. The sun began to set. At that time I awoke from the lovely dream. I felt so secure and comforted. I ran home to my mother. I found her preparing food. I refused to eat until we had fed the poor. The next morning I helped my family look after the garden, clean the street and plant trees. I have told all my friends of the dream and they are now cooperative. The strong help the weak and the rich help the poor.

Renda Mosia Salim Albreem, Age 14, Jordan

As the family forms the basic unit of society, its principles, when rightly emphasized, will do much to bring a better world for all peoples.

Pastor David E. Hay, Mission Secretary, Tonga

For a better world, the family, the fundamental element of society, must keep stable. Relationships between individuals must be based on the love of the family.

Ji-Gon Leong, Professor, Republic of Korea

It would be a pleasure to see a world full of love and harmony. I'd like to see the number of broken marriages reduce to zero and be sure that children were free from abuse. I would like to see the world as a community.

Alice Kingori, Student, Age 16, Kenya

In a better world love is the basis of family life. In that family there will always be peace and calmness and so it will be like a refuge or a safe port. There will be a constructive dialogue taking place, creating more understanding amongst family members. The bond between family members will be deep and the gap between generations will not exist. Parents will not have any preferences concerning the sex of their children. They will inspire their children to develop their own individuality, not imposing their own ideals. Children will not feel that they are controlled by their parents because the parents will guide them with discretion and through their own example. Children will accept their advice since parents will observe the principles they teach.

Roundtable Group, Student Nurses, Greece

For the happiness of the family it is important to change some traditional men's practices, so there is more freedom and happiness for women. The world would be better if women could have greater participation in the management of the world.

Sena Sekulic-Gvozdanovic, Professor, Croatia

The most important cell in society is the family. If the family is good, the country is also good.

Edward Camilleri, Malta

"Global Cooperation for a Better World", Juana Ruiz Kolb, Germany

In a better world we would have better parents.

Jyoti, Student, India

The family, as part of the international community, brings up children for the sake of the whole world and all the people.

Karen V. Issraelyan, Student, Russia

Our families reflect the environment and the social circumstances and development of the community. We live in houses arranged like a cluster of flowers which facilitates the mutual assistance of families. Mono-parent families, in particular, help each other. There is mutual understanding between family members of different generations. Domestic tasks are fulfilled in a harmonious manner and each family incorporates a sense of unity.

Roundtable Group, Switzerland

"Peace is...Love", Giovanna Lacorty, Switzerland

As a politician, my dream is to work for a world where all people feel good, starting from the family/group we belong to. Harmony and balance within the small 'nucleus' from where we start the day gives us the power to go beyond borders and work towards more happiness for all people.

Wivina Demeester-De Meyer, Minister, Belgium

My vision of a better world is one in which every child born could expect to be loved by those close to her, respected by all others, to have her physical, social and intellectual needs met by her family and her society and to have no limitations placed on her pursuit of creative and spiritual fulfillment. It would be a world which will expect from her an offering of her gifts and talents toward the enrichment of her community, and her world and toward an exchange of special gifts and capacities with others, within and outside her community, so that the fullness and diversity of the human family might be enjoyed and enhanced, and others perceived as a source of such human richness.

Betty Reardon, Peace Educator, USA

In a world centred on God as a parent, people relate as brothers and sisters, thereby constituting a global family.

James Egadu, Student, Uganda

"My dharma is to work so that I can give": This philosophy of our father Parmanand Deepchand Hinduja (1901-1962), founder of the Hinduja Group, inspired by the Holy Gita's precept that "charity must come from within as an expression of an irrepressible urge of one's own heart", has been the guiding light of my family. Our father believed that good health and education were the fundamental rights of every human being, and dedicated himself to this belief. Our beloved mother Jamuna followed him devoutly. His sympathy for the afflicted, his belief in the spirit of progress and the truth of his religious teaching that good always prevails and flourishes has continued to inspire our actions.

Srichand P. Hinduja, Chairman, UK

"Playing After Raining", Isabel Gouveia, Portugal

In a better world, people commit themselves to a new solidarity, the solidarity of the human family.

Tuulikki Juusela, Managing Director, Finland

The woman and the family. To take my own example - my husband used to be a high-ranking executive working on average 20 hour days. On taking his invalid father into our home he decided to leave outside work and work independently. Now he works at home and I have also started to work increasingly from the home. This has led me to think that perhaps now, with the enormous development in electronic devices, some of the splintering of the home which has occurred because of the industrial revolution can be reversed. I think the key to this is to bring the workplace back into the home. This makes it easier for both the father and mother to be with the children and to share the homemaking between them, without having to give up a career or a profession.

Alice Shalvi, Educator, Israel

In my opinion, a woman is first a mother, wife or sister and later a career woman. When a woman gets married she learns to be adjusting and loving. As a mother, she is caring and affectionate and as a sister most accommodating and sincere. When a family woman goes out to the professional front, she makes use of her virtues so deftly that clearly she becomes the most loved colleague. As a worker she is efficient and firm yet gentle, a hard taskmaster yet supple and above all extremely loving.

Capt. Nivedita Bhasin, Airline Pilot, India

Let us join in a world-wide celebration of the unity of the human family to mark the Year of Interreligious Understanding and Cooperation. Let us give thanks that with the wonderful variety of different races, colours, languages, religions and customs, we belong to one family. It is an occasion to renew our efforts to ensure fullness of life for all members of that family.

Rev. Marcus Braybrooke, Clergyman, UK

A world in which our children are viewed as our treasures and our elders are honoured as teachers.

Betsy Herbert, Educational Consultant, USA

Family life would be based on a real partnership of parents and children. Parents ought to try to understand new ways of living in a rapidly changing world; only thus may the generation gap be overcome.

Teresa Truszkowska, Poet, Poland

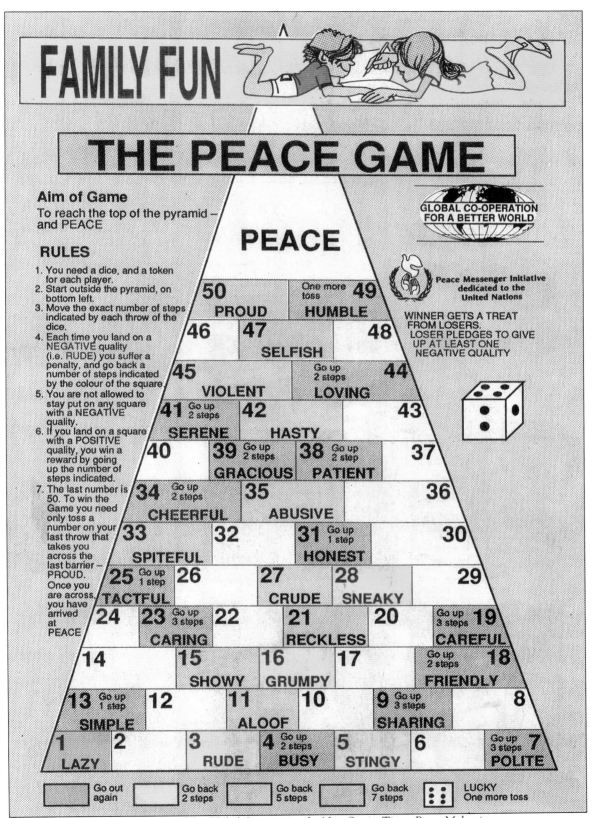

Published in Malaysian Sunday Mail for Global Cooperation by New Straits Times Press, Malaysia

"Light Rhythm", Geeta Ramparsad, Mauritius

In a Better World:

There is respect, understanding and tolerance in all human relations.

人际关系充满尊重、理解和忍让。

Люди относятся друг к другу с уважением, пониманием и терпимостью.

Le respect, la compréhension et la tolérance règnent dans toutes les relations humaines.

يسود الاحترام والتفاهم والتسامح جميع العلاقات الإنسانية.

Hay respeto, comprensión y tolerancia en todas las relaciones humanas.

7 RESPECT, UNDERSTANDING AND TOLERANCE

If all people would give respect to their neighbours and understand their own and others' values, the world would improve. Values like tolerance and patience are very important in life.

Roundtable Group, Zimbabwe

A better world will never exist without the will, the determination that makes human beings turn towards one another, to accept their differences as opportunities for the future. Love and tolerance are far from being just empty words. They are the instigators of the will for harmony that spreads little by little upon the planet. They are voices that unite and sing the same song, above everything that separates them.

Yves Duteil, Artist, France

I would like the world to be a place where we could find peace, understanding, tolerance, less selfishness; where we could give ourselves to others, help one another and live with love.

Olga Arellano Salgado, Professor, Chile

Whether white or black, right or left the hearts are the same. The glow of life is not in the glitter of gold but in human love.

D. S. Sheriff, Professor, Libya

I would like to see a world with universal citizens, i.e. everyone is equal in the eyes of the world.

K. K. Dass, Teacher, Singapore

You'll see the world around you
in lovely rainbow hues.
Just open up your heart
and wear your brother's shoes.
Veronica Gould, Housewife, Canada

Hickory Dickory Dock,
The world is like a clock,
If we tick together,
We can live forever,
Hickory Dickory Dock.
Mark Hoskin, Child, Australia

Reboti Bhusan
Ghosh, India

Kids Cooperation, a mural painted on an underpass in Redditch, UK, by children aged 8-14 following a Global Cooperation Creative Group.

Living and studying one year with people from all different nationalities, races, professions and religions, I discovered that all human beings have basically the same desires and aspirations; that there exist respect and friendship if we all concentrate more on the things that unite us instead of those that separate us. This can come about with patience, tolerance and understanding. On these experiences I base my trust and optimism that we will see the day when all human beings would consider themselves to be true brothers living on planet Earth.

Carmen Mesones Villacorta, Chemist, Peru

Progressive historical, cultural, moral and religious traditions and customs of all the nations and ethnic groups should be equally respected and defended. They should have free choice of the given possibilities and the right to further development in their own way.

Laszlo Kozma, Physicist, Hungary

I want a united world, committed to keeping peace, but not at the expense of the individuality of different cultures.

Briar Middleditch, Puppet-Maker, New Zealand

We think that differences between cultures should be acknowledged and different approaches to reality accepted. The main task seems to be removing barriers of distrust and fear between people and nations and eradicating egoism at all levels and in every disguise. Our vision of the world is the world free from ideologies of any kind.

L. Drozdik, Professor, Slovakia

Scrape away our fear, open hearts of friendship will appear.

Fred Segal, Businessman, USA

Relationships between people must be sincere. They must be based on faith in the self, and in the human beings with whom you communicate. People must have a slogan: It will be good for me when it is good for everyone.

Boris Mineev, Age 15, Russia

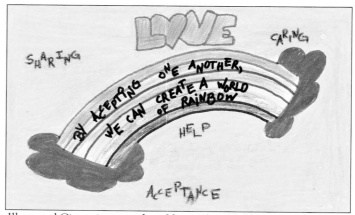

Illustrated Cinquain poem, Jane Venus, Age 16, Micronesia

"La Festa Dell' Arcobaleno", Santocchi Paola and Todini Graziella, Italy

My vision is that of a world bathed in celestial light of spiritualism, wherein one will see God in every other person and worship him as he would worship God. That is the way of Indian saints, whereby colour, caste, creed, religion, poverty, superiority, inferiority - everything vanishes. What remains is the LIGHT OF LOVE - radiant and celestial.

Ramanand Sagar, Producer, Director and Writer, India

The world is rich in variety, but there is no superior race, creed or culture. When we accept this, we shall be able to cooperate for a better world.

Elsie Tu, Legislative Councillor, Hong Kong

I will be tolerant towards those who have a different opinion or look different to me.

Lieve Vandekerckhove, Student, Belgium

Everyone should feel that he is not just responsible for self and family, but he is a man who is part of a universal group of people and he has to do what he can to provide equality. The basis of your life is that you love every human being as yourself and have a commitment towards people, the country and the entire world.

Rabbi Schlomo Goren, Chief Rabbi, Israel

A world governed by a profound respect for other people, for objects and for nature. In such a world, respect - in its Latin meaning of "act of looking back", heeding the other - should ban violence, envy and the other taints which now poison human relationships.

Thomas Kleininger, Publisher, Romania

From the Global Cooperation Art Contest "My Idea of a Better World", Hong Kong, Leon Men King, Age 13, Hong Kong

People associate with each other in a light, intuitive and natural way, free from claims and expectations. Relationships are accepted as they come because people live completely present in the moment. People are not judged or classified. Relationships are not to satisfy a deficiency, but to express the inner richness of a loving heart.

Roundtable Group, Germany

There would be respect for the sovereignty and independence of all nations regardless of physical size or economic strength.

P.T. Timeon, Secretary for Foreign Affairs, Kiribati

There would be peaceful coexistence and cooperation at local, national and international levels.

Du Yaoguo, Dean, China

I am coming more and more to feel that a key issue is how to encourage and create attitudes that differences are good and should be encouraged - while at the same time avoiding the multitude of destructive conflicts that they lead to. We can teach people to be more understanding, accepting of, and even appreciative of differences.

Barry Childers, Psychologist, Switzerland

We might have an American President come to Japan and have a soak in hot springs or something like that to feel closer. We wouldn't have the feeling that they belong to that world and we are different.

Student, Japan

Sons of the World
Why don't you hold hands now?
Stand together united;
Rebuild our world in harmony;
Work together as small children.
They forgive and forget
Why don't you do the same?
Forget about the skin colour;
Forget about past oppressions;
Accept the present.
And plan for a good future.

*Bernadette Nyekete,
Student, Zimbabwe*

Mari Carmen Camacho, Age 14, Spain

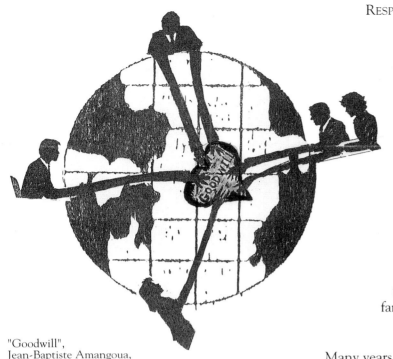

"Goodwill",
Jean-Baptiste Amangoua,
Cote d'Ivoire

You ask how I see a "better world". I believe we were created for a world in a delicate network of relationships - divine and human; nature animate and inanimate - fundamentally relationships of inter-dependence, where rights of humans and those of creation are recognized and respected. Where people are seen to be created for fellowship, not alienation and estrangement. Where they are recognized as endowed intrinsically with infinite worth because they are created in the image of God and are therefore all members of one family, the human family - God's family.

Archbishop Desmond M. Tutu, South Africa

Many years ago a European asked me what African humanity was. I promptly told him that African humanity was not different from European humanity - the essence of being in man. Humanity could not therefore be labelled according to continents or races.

My experience has shown me more clearly than ever before that there is no single heart in the world that does not throb for love and understanding and for a better life than that offered by their various governments. And this common desire can only be realized under conditions of peace, love and cooperation among nations.

Gabriel Okara, Poet and Novelist, Nigeria

I think I'd have very long, brown hair,
which I could sit on when I was on a chair,
I would be kind, I would be helpful,
I'd help people when they were not well,
I think I'd be the funniest of all
and I'd be very tall.
I'd want to be friends with everyone
so we could play and all have fun.
I'd never be selfish, or rude or unkind,
and always keep others in mind.
Do unto others as you would have them do to you,
Because that is a saying that has always been true,
A better me is what I'd like to be.

Claire Pinel, Child, UK

"We want to be friends!", Lieve Van Herck, Belgium

I can think of no greater objectives for any man or woman than to be kind and generous to fellow human beings and to members of the animal kingdom as well.

It is easy to be kind to those we both like and respect but far more difficult to deal with those we find unattractive or even unpleasant. But quick judgements can often be wrong and a warm heart can be concealed by a harsh and prickly skin. It is the effort we make that is important to us. What does it matter if someone considers you an easy touch? It is more important that you have done your best.

"We all Love Peace", winner of Third Prize, Junior Section, in the Global Cooperation Art Contest, "My Idea of a Better World", Hong Kong, Chui Chan Yu, Age 8, Hong Kong

Generosity does not mean carelessly handing out your time and finance to anyone who asks. It involves careful investigation and sound judgement. But it also means being ready to err on the side of those who may not be so convincing. Even if someone has misled you in the past a little generosity now may turn the tide for them. And if you are proved wrong at least you will have tried. But don't be foolishly generous - that may well harm both you and the recipient.

Sir Edmund Hillary, New Zealand

"Everyone asks you to help them. They want love, harmony and peace", Elisabeth Martinez Escala, Age 12, Spain

"My Better World",
Aminah Ahmed Rahshid,
Jordan

Enrique Santamaria and Ruth Ramirez,
Spain

I was taught at school never to describe any age in history as "an age of transition." It is a lesson I have always remembered, and whenever I am tempted to suggest that we live in an age of change, I always remember that admonition from my youth.

Yet, despite the risks of using the term, I believe ours is an age seeing changes which bring hope rather than instability. I sense it in the new cordiality between East and West, and the desire for peace among nations which is such a prominent feature of the philosophy of many young people. I see it too in the upsurge of concern for the natural world and the welfare of our planet. This gives me great hope because I believe that learning to conserve the delicate balance of nature informs our perception of how we should treat each other. As we learn to understand the interdependence of natural things, so we learn that we too are interdependent beings.

I pray that as we develop this reverence for our neighbours and for our surroundings, we might also grow in our belief that cooperation is a fundamental principle of human life. Competition is not, as is sometimes thought, the only spur to developing our gifts and talents.

The Rt. Rev. Robert Runcie, UK

"Village Scene", Benson Nzali, Zimbabwe

In a Better World:

People communicate openly and in a spirit of equality and goodwill.

人人本着平等及和善的精神，彼此坦诚地交流。

В общении люди открыты, благожелательны и ровны.

Chacun communique ouvertement et dans un esprit d'égalité et de bonne volonté.

يكـون الاتصـال بـين النـاس منفتحا، وفي روح من المساواة وحسن النية.

Las personas se comunican abiertamente y en un espiritu de igualdad y de buena voluntad.

8 COMMUNICATING WITH GOODWILL

We will communicate beyond words, and words will be a kind of music, a game. Contacts between each other will be an art and creation of beauty.

Creative Group, Poland

I would like a world where people communicate on the basis of equality and their relationships are based on honesty and self-knowledge.

Margarita Diamantopoulou, Civil Servant, Greece

Honesty, love for the self, the ability to listen to and understand others are some of the ingredients to make better communication and a world of trust a reality.

Roundtable Group, Australia

When exchanging information on any social occasion, people respect an inner code of conduct resulting in a natural form of ethics. Communication is focused on doing things together, creating and being together.

Roundtable Group, Belgium

I see communication and information, based on the principles of genuine participation and interpersonal communication within nation states, and among and between nations, as providing the framework for positive change and a guarantee of freedom for all.

Ed Fung, TV Producer, Trinidad & Tobago

We should continue to be able to sit around tables with open minds, to hold dialogues and discourses in the increasingly globalized market place of ideas. These free exchanges of ideas are necessary for the betterment of the human condition. The free passage of ideas between nations should be encouraged. We need to know more about each other in order to understand each other.

Raja Noora Ashikin Binti Raja Abdullah, Stockbroker, Malaysia

"Peace Among Different Cultures", Constantin Nicolas, Mauritius

Children, age 10, at Rynkeby Lille School, Denmark, express their vision of a better world in words, wax models and paintings while playing "The Game of the World". (Berit Svensson, Denmark)

Everyone can communicate from the heart and everyone has an open mind. Everyone sees others at all times with equal eyes.

Mitsuko Takada, Student, Japan

If each of us, in all fields of life, could speak, write, think, listen and act from our hearts, would we not touch the sensitivity of many? Would we not touch some people's souls, and see how their hearts blossom like flowers in spring?

Valentin Alejandro Ladra, Journalist, Venezuela

I think that what people need more than anything else is love and truth plus of course real uninhibited communication between individuals and nations. It sounds simple enough but if you take it seriously there is enormous work to be done along these lines. We all can contribute towards a better world.

Vladimir Ashkenazy, Musician, Switzerland

I believe that a better world awaits us. It will be facilitated when barriers, walls, borders are broken down. Every effort should be put towards a better communication of values, ideas and cultures. To achieve this, people from different parts of the world should know more of each other, should see more of each other and understand each other.

Mustafa Artvinli, Professor, Turkey

The means of communication are as universal as possible with respect for each individual and within the cultural and ethical traditions of each person.

Roundtable Group, Italy

Art is a universal language through which people of all nations can communicate. It enables humanity to rise above political and philosophical differences. Its force is so powerful that it provides the seed of true understanding and binds humankind through a common energy bringing us closer to world peace.

Vuong Nhi Chiem, Vietnam

News-making should be true and correct, no more, no less.

Farshad Ravaei, Engineer, Iran

"The Bridge of Harmony": Youth in Thailand find out more about the art of cooperation by together building a symbolic bridge of harmony. (Somphong Bunthirasmi, Thailand)

Young Cooperators at the Global Cooperation Exhibition Stand, Belgium. (Danny Puype, Belgium)

Develop intercultural-communication.

Falilou Diallo, Coordinator, Senegal

All newspapers should instantly set aside those lines of accidents and crimes and instead have a column of "goodwill" followed by practical examples.

Hedwig Fincke, Age 94, Germany

In a better world, all people easily understand each other. They communicate without language barriers. Besides their native mother languages all of them speak an auxiliary international language.

Anatoly Ionesov, Museum Director, Uzbekistan

I see a world with much peace, where everyone gets along with each other. I would love to see a world with one language. This is why there isn't peace, because we don't understand each other. I would like to see a world with one language no matter which one it is.

Celia Cruz, Singer, Cuba

Communication in the better future world is one that gives free access to, and use of, all types of information resources for all. There would be the instant translation and transmission of information, ideas, experiences, art and expression. This would be very important to the different ethno-linguistic groups in a global-village context.

Roundtable Group, Philippines

The objective of the media is to educate, to express the culture of people and the arts, and to inspire people to have a wider consciousness. The strength of the message is in its quality and not in its quantity. The message is positive, catching and makes the listener feel good.

Roundtable Group, Spain

Let there be an international law for better communication between nations; this law must have principles of equality and justice between the big and small countries.

Mahdi Muhsin Al-Obaidi, Iraq

Dadi Prakashmani, Administrative Head of the Brahma Kumaris and President of Global Cooperation's International Advisory Committee, shares a light moment with Committee Co-Chair James Jonah, Under-Secretary-General, United Nations. (W. Nowakowski, Australia)

Media should earnestly educate the people to think for themselves by clarifying issues to develop informed opinions, to appreciate the problems of other human beings and come up with solutions to them.

The mass media should be the conscience of society in taking up issues such as exploitation of workers and consumers; corruption; plight of the poor and the disadvantaged; people's access to health, education and housing facilities; the despoiling of the environment; the anti-drug campaign; racism; decolonization; disarmament; the nonaligned movement; and cooperation among states for mutual economic development.

As powerful potential change agents in society, all journalists and communicators in general should sincerely seek to exert through their work such influences as can generate among their audiences informed opinions and positive thoughts and perceptions of themselves, other people and the world about them. Such an approach, even through suggested role models projected in the media, can dramatically influence for the better our day to day human relations.

Reporters thus need to rethink what makes news and re-examine the inherited but irrelevant news values, in the context today of the growing enlightened recognition that communication is a process and that news itself is process-oriented rather than the mere recounting of events. Reporters should deal with contentious and conflict issues with a nicety that focuses on those cultural and related elements that unite rather on those that divide society.

By sensible selection and studied distribution of reportorial material without any censorship, reporters and editors alike should help provide the vehicle for popular sampling of, and respect for, different views and multimedia which should be predominantly privately owned.

Public communication schools and the media organizations themselves should introduce and sustain a national educational programme of journalistic reorientation and retraining. This is to help develop in media workers the ability to communicate with a deep sensitivity to the effect that their words and deeds are likely to have on their captive audiences.

In the ideally multiparty democracies, where state-owned media operate alongside increasing private ownership, media organizations themselves should aggressively lobby for the setting up of a constitution to protect the media messages from political interferences. This should leave the mass media free to promote constructive criticism; worthwhile cultural and spiritual values of society; and the spirit of universal brotherhood in the sense of creative cooperativism. And so, the avant-garde journalist uniquely uses a vision of the future and not the violence of the past to change the present.

Victor Forsythe,
Media Communication Consultant,
Guyana

"How to Achieve
a Better World?",
Unknown,
Spain

A journalist is not objective, he has ideas and feelings, happy moments and fears. But the main value is to be objective, to try to describe and work on a topic and interview people in an objective way. You have to be honest with yourself, you cannot interfere. You are the instrument to convey the message of the situation or the person to the public.

To know the slant of the journalist before you read him or her requires an intelligent and educated audience. There is a necessity to be able to discriminate between the information and the opinion of the journalist. It depends on the task of the journalist, whether they are acting as a reporter, an interpreter or an editor. Today we tend to mix between the factual and editorial opinion and this is very dangerous. If you talk in terms of a good media, you should know exactly where the report begins and ends, where the editorial begins and ends, and where the opinion is being given. Journalism has to stick to facts when reporting. When you are interpreting you take the facts that you like. Good media is first of all information. Information is facts and figures. What is built is the result of this. If you mix facts and opinions it is bad journalism.

The audience is reading and watching in their leisure

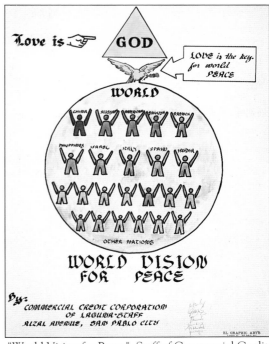

"World Vision for Peace", Staff of Commercial Credit Corp. of Laguna, Philippines

hours so to some extent you have to give the audience something entertaining. Instead of educating or leading your audience to what they should be seeing, in your opinion, you are entertaining them by giving them what they want to see. This is the commercial side of the media and is having an increasing influence on journalism.

You are also the eyes and the ears of the person sitting at home, remote from the person or situation you are describing. It has the value of entertainment, but the basic responsibility is to bring the information to the public. Journalism plays a great role in making people understand each other as individuals and as nations.

In every country there is some form of selection in terms of the press. The right of the people to know is the basic value of journalism, and the minute that there is censorship there is not true freedom to know. In an ideal situation all news that is fit to print should be printed. The choice should be open to the public to develop their own opinions and reactions about the subject material.

When people talk about a better world, the question is which type of journalism is influencing the world. Local journalism and local television is almost dead. We are talking today about global communications. Communication is one of the strongest powers to help bring about a better world.

Zivia Cohen, Magazine Editor, Israel

My vision of a better world is a world in which man can live as one, think as one and feel for each other, a world in which the different languages are used to promote harmony, a world in which it is a pleasure to share views with others and a world in which selflessness and living for others take precedence over all else.

John Nkomo, Govt. Minister, Zimbabwe

"Peace", Miss Daina Tahseen Bolooh, Jordan

In a Better World:

Social, economic and political justice is ensured through honesty, responsibility and respect for the rule of law.

依靠诚实、责任心和对法治的尊重来保证社会、经济和政治的公平。

Честные, ответственные отношения между людьми, уважение к закону гарантируют социальную, экономическую и политическую справедливость.

Chacun communique ouvertement et dans un esprit d'égalité et de bonne volonté.

تؤمن العدالـة الاقتصاديـة والسياسـية بـواسـطة الأمانـة والمسؤولية وإحترام حكم القانون.

La justicia social, económica y politica se garantiza mediante la honestidad, la responsabilidad y el respeto al imperio de la ley.

9 JUSTICE AND LAW

In God's Laws we trust.

Benouar Djillali, Scientist, Algeria

I believe we should strive to move toward a world in which relations among nations would be based on the rule of law, supported by a system of collective security, with conflict resolution and peace-keeping functions performed by multi-lateral institutions.

Robert S. McNamara, USA

There would be a new, international economic legal system in which all nations and individuals have the same opportunities; where no one takes advantage of any other; and where the basic needs of each individual (both material and spiritual) are met.

Ismail Chaban, Economist, Syria

If all leaders, politicians, etc are honest with themselves, their colleagues and subordinates, there will be trust, cooperation and hard work on the part of every individual and in no time the political, social and economic problems of the world will be solved.

J. A. Aghenta, Professor, Nigeria

In a better world there would be stable peace for all nations. Every country would have independence, liberation, democracy and happiness.

Ho Xuan Thanh, Engineer, Vietnam

Reverence for sovereignty of independent states. Economic fairness, justice and tolerance towards less economically advanced independent states.

Allan Marat, Legal Practitioner, Papua New Guinea

Each country should have the freedom to decide on the economic model which is most convenient to the particular conditions of each nation, according to their historical tradition, degree of development and the areas of geopolitical influence which they are in.

Jaime Fernando Pineda Sosa, Civil Servant, Guatemala

"Unity", Melanie Jastillana, Micronesia

The primary task of each state should be the creation of a legal and economic environment capable of guaranteeing the minimum to the needy, but first of all able to create working and business possibilities for citizens without any limitation.

Borislav Ivosevic, Professor, Yugoslavia

People of the world should recognize that uplifting standards of living and income for everybody is a legitimate aspiration.

Amara Raksasataya, Professor, Thailand

Everyone considers that business contributes positively to society. There is an easy exchange of goods, services and ideas through which the needs of all citizens are met. Technology and goods may be readily exported anywhere in the world. Consumers are responsible and do not make demands in excess of their needs. People in business are good citizens and set good examples. They have self-respect, respect for others, honesty, strength and leadership. People are our primary resource. Business exchanges are like an exchange between family members.

Roundtable Group, Business Executives, Switzerland

There is production according to capacity and consumption according to one's needs.

Creative Group, Netherlands

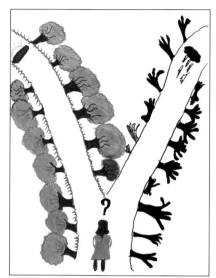

"A New World", Evani Santanna, Age 12, Brazil

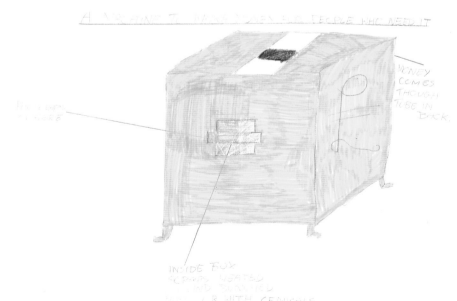

A machine to make money for people who need it, Pupil, Coston School, UK

Employment is not based on paper qualifications but proficiency in the skills needed. As each person pursues his career according to his skills, competition is non-existent. There is mutual respect and recognition of each one's contribution towards the success of the organization in which they are employed. Good working conditions, with a management concerned for the welfare and safety of the employees, naturally enhances productivity.

Bart Willems, Belgium

Creative Group, Malaysia

In our future world the value of money will be real, based on the amount of work that was necessary to create this value. Just salaries are given for mental as well as physical work, and evaluation is made according to the responsibility you carry and your own efforts. Everyone has enough money to reach a good social standard by doing work which is useful to people and the economy as a whole.

Roundtable Group, Austria

All countries will respect the currency of all other countries, to create such a situation in which active international trade can be done.

Stoytcho Stoev, Professor, Bulgaria

As an economist, I believe that world economic systems should be held together by an overarching principle which combines freedom with responsibility and justice with compassion.

Syed Nawab Haider Naqvi, Economist, Pakistan

Tiana Templeman, Australia

My vision is that the soul and conscience of law and justice would reflect the soul and conscience of those who administer the law and justice and if they are spiritually inspired and/or motivated, then law and justice will be just.

Ramesh Lawrence Maharaj, Attorney at Law, Trinidad & Tobago

I am looking forward to see the solution of all differences between governments by international courts of justice.

Michail Maratheftis, Author, Cyprus

One should not steal, but be honest and ask. One should obey the rules and know what is right and what is wrong.

Sandra Munshi, Suriname

Artwork painted for "The Windows Project" in which shop-front windows were whitewashed and used as a canvas by students to launch the Spoleto Fringe Festival, Melbourne. Randall Boyce, Australia

A value system which sustains the human community and is sustained by the consensus of the people as a whole is known as Dharma. It is a compound of righteousness, social justice and injunctions of good behaviour which preserve a community's integrity. Lawlessness is disorder and law breeds order provided it is vitalized by the values of righteousness and community-oriented justice.

V. R. Krishna Iyer,
Former Judge, India

A world in which the equality of human beings becomes a reality and a person is judged, not by politics, religion, culture or the colour of skin, but by the quality of spirit. A world in which there is peace, freedom and justice for all.

Sir William Keys, Company Director, Australia

I would like there to be more insistence on the necessity of a profound honesty from everybody at whatever level they may be found.

Anne-Marie Le Bot, Librarian, Mali

Individually, and as a nation, we must encourage the establishment of truly democratic governments respectful of the rule of law and of basic human rights. We must assist, to the extent possible, in the creation of economies in which people can not only satisfy their basic needs, but also realize their full potential.

Dante B. Fascell, Former Congressman, USA

People participate in electing the legislators, the leaders and the enforcement officers and are actively involved in the discussions that go into law making. People therefore see that it is in fact their law not a ruler's law that has been enacted. And since the people will legislate into law only those customs of which they approve and understand there is little likelihood of extreme ignorance of its provisions even in the most unconcerned citizen among them.

Moses Gitau & Richard Kariuki, Lawyers, Kenya

"One Family", Tomasz Jagodzinski, Age 13, Poland

My vision of the future sees a rising of dominance of honesty as a feature, not just in the context of crime reduction and diminution of deceit but in our daily dealings with each other and our analyses of ourselves. Character weaknesses, ranging from timidity and uncertainty, through insensitivity and selfishness to arrogance, will be admitted to ourselves and their impact upon others in the community will be offset by conscious efforts to achieve a proper balance.

I visualize everyone in the community striving to promote justice for all - locally and globally. The thoughts, motivations and guiding influences in all our minds will be predominantly altruistic.

A. G. Lynn, Chief Constable, UK

Global Cooperation Artwork, India

I see the Year 2001, I am quarter of a century old
The head of the United Nations -
my story has been told in movies, books and
magazines, how I saved the world from war
when I wrote to the superpowers, back in 1994.
I sent the leaders a boomerang,
with a message I had to give:
"Here's a symbol from Down Under,
from a boy who wants to live.
Before you plunge the world in darkness,
please give some thought at length
to the fact that your deeds, good or bad,
return to you with strength.
As ye sow so shall ye reap,
will you give to the world, or take?
Peace and love is the better crop -
the choice is yours to make."
They heeded my humble message,
then I travelled countries strange,
spreading the message of the boomerang,
and the world began to change.
People extended the hand of friendship,
prejudice was swept away
All religions and races knocked down their walls,
joining hands to pray to all their gods,
one mighty force, to put goodness in every heart.

Greed and corruption disappeared,
that was a healthy start!
Material wealth was shared around,
and crime was next to go.
Bad drugs and firearms were destroyed,
the smart folk helped the slow.
With my family's help I made a plan,
for all nations to combine
and share resources as one world.
Soon the U.N.'s head office was mine.
And the boomerang is the world symbol,
our aim is goodness - straight and true.
And our motto: "Your deeds, good or bad,
come back, with strength, to you."

Sam Thorne, Age 11, Australia
(Winner of "My Idea for a Better World" Contest)

"Fiesta", Robert Llimos, Spain

We are on the verge of a transition from one world economic order to another - a fundamental shift that has the potential of bringing about one of the most exciting periods in human history. For most of this century, the industrialized countries succeeded by taking natural resources out of the ground - oil, wheat, coal - adding manufacturing know-how to those resources and turning them into products. Then, they developed services around these new products.

In a very short time we have seen a dramatic change in that economic system. Today we are no longer in the Industrial Age. We are in an information-intensive, global dynamic economy. The resources are no longer just those that come out of the ground. The resources today come out of our minds. They are ideas and information.

This trend has huge implications in terms of the workplace of the future and what jobs will be available for people around the world.

In the 1920s, Henry Ford set up mass production at the Ford Motor Company and industrial engineer Frederick Taylor defined work in a way that would make mass production efficient. The concept was relatively simple. He broke down work to the simplest possible task so that the worker at the lowest level of the hierarchy was expected to have no particular skill or knowledge. Tasks became so simple that almost anybody could perform them. Then, there were a series of managers or supervisors above that individual, and each level would check the work of the level below.

Separately, organizations would have a staff organization to do all of the thinking, analysis, planning, forecasting, and budgeting. These parallel organizations have been the structure of our industrial economy, and have provided the strength for mass producers around the world.

Today, line people are doing their own staff work. Hierarchies are collapsing as people communicate electronically. One of the next big ideas in the reorganization of work will be collaboration. People will be working together in small teams on a common task. Electronic Mail lets people work in "task-teams" without physically getting together, and they can work at a time convenient to each team member.

In the 1990s, management priorities for organizations will be very different from the 1980s. Work is becoming more competitive, segmented and task-oriented. People will assemble electronically in task-teams to solve problems. More and more, college graduates are being put on the factory floor, because they're able to combine the staff and the line jobs. People at the lowest levels of the organization have to possess the thinking skills to make judgments and decisions about such things as when to make a change on the product line or when to order more components.

The point is that we are living in a global economy where workers will need a different quality of education to prepare them for these jobs. As a result, they're able to turn out products that are of higher quality at a lower cost. This reorganization of work also has important implications on the style and effectiveness of leadership. Instead of emulating the autocratic, invincible leadership models of the past, successful managers will be those who lead by inspiring individuals, by empowering them to make decisions and ultimately to make a meaningful difference in the organization.

Empowerment is often seen as something one can "do" to another person. This is not so. People are empowered by an environment that gives them the freedom to express themselves as freely as they can. Leadership is about creating such an environment enabling others to become creative managers in their own right. In this new world of work, individuals are asked to pour a part of themselves into the success of the enterprise with which they're associated. Individuals are asked for a greater commitment than in the days when they were simply a cog in the wheel of a systematized corporation. In return, people should get an experience that sharpens their instincts, teaches them the newest lessons, shows them how to become self-engaged in their work, and gives them new ways of looking at the world. This does not mean open-ended loyalty. While they are in an organization, people have to buy into the vision that guides it. Unlike any other time in history, the availability and accessibility of information is making it possible for individuals to have a clear understanding of an organization's vision and what they must do to make it a reality.

John Sculley, Chairman and CEO, USA

Our global vision must and should consider the idea of a harmonious social order in every society so that every human being in any particular society should be insulated against tyranny and discrimination and have equal opportunities in the fields of education, health and wealth from or of that society.

Ben K. Kuma, Industrialist, Ghana

I believe the best system for the global future is the system where all individuals create the system collectively. The principles in society give everyone equal opportunity.

Brahim El Kadiri Boutchich, Lecturer, Morocco

Eleonu Chimene, Nigeria

In a Better World:

Governments, as representatives of their people, are committed to their well-being.
People participate cooperatively in efforts for a secure and peaceful world.

政府作为人民的代表致力于为人民谋福利。 人民共同参
与为建立一个安全及和平的世界而努力。

Правительства выражают интересы своих народов, заботятся об
их благосостоянии. Люди активно участвуют в строительстве
мира, свободного от страха и войн.

Les gouvernements, représentant leurs peuples, s'engagent à leur assurer
le bien-être. Chacun participe conjointement aux efforts pour bâtir un monde
sûr et pacifique.

الحكومات كممثلين لشعوبهم، يلتزمون بخير حياتهم. ويشارك
الناس متعاونين في جهودهم نحو عالم آمن ومسالم.

Los gobiernos defienden el bienestar de su pueblo, del que son
representantes. Las personas cooperan en los esfuerzos por un mundo seguro y
pacifico.

10 DEMOCRATIC GOVERNMENT AND PEOPLE PARTICIPATION

Ordinary people would serve in the government.
Student, Japan

There is no conflict between people and people, nation and nation, country and country. People all dedicate themselves to the development and happy causes of the whole world.

Lin Ji Ken, Professor, China

Governments used to be called public servants. They are the servants of the public. It is not the public who serve you; it is you who serve them. The intentions of whoever thought of these things were right, were noble, but it is how we have used them that has resulted in a public official becoming someone people fear or disregard.

What is a government? It is us, it is me; it is we who make the government. Where you find human rights have been violated it is because a government thinks that this is my right - I can give it to the people or I can keep it to myself. That's where the problem lies. There are the laws and the laws have to be enforced by the government but the government is an instrument. What right has the government to say that so and so is entitled to something but you are not?

People and government will work together when they know the people are the government and the government is the people. It is not that governments have anything to give but they are there to do what the people want them to do. A government can seek to enable people to live peacefully, to develop to their utmost ability. A government should realize that it is there to enable things to happen. They are not there for people to buy things from them, for me to buy my rights from you. How much did you pay for it that I should buy it from you?

Anon., Kenya

"Unity is Strength", Teacher and pupils of St. George's Nursery School, Guyana

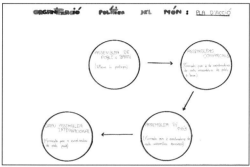

Creative Group, Bonastree School, Spain

I would like to see every person, organization and government participating in conflict resolution programmes, and developing, learning and implementing conflict resolution skills.

Stella Cornelius, Director, Australia

There will be a time that most governments will be true representatives of their people. The will of the people will conquer all kinds of dictatorship.

Ali Afrooz, Dean, Iran

In a better world there would be a Peoples' United Nations, rather than the present one which is based on states. A Peoples' UN would have groups based on common interests, missions, and on problems that are seeking solutions. A Peoples' UN would have people talking about their concerns rather than expressing their governments' stands.

Fatimah Hamid-Don, Retired, Malaysia

My vision of a better world would be one under the control of a strong United Nations, one that truly had the support of all countries in the world. The devastation caused by war and the pollution of our environment knows no boundaries. Only an effective, united world government could provide sufficient law and have the power to control these destructive forces.

Lloyd Bridges, Actor, USA

Our vision is of a government which would be just, responsible and dedicated to the welfare of the state. The image is of a parent role rather than that of an alienated, isolated institution.

Roundtable Group, University Students, Bangladesh

The policies of governments worldwide should put more emphasis and consideration on general human values.

I. Sajkova, Professor, Bulgaria

All governments must be accountable to the people. There should be a supreme world government. It is high time the world took responsibility for its people rather than continue with each country's self-styled government systems in which we have assortments very similar to those in a large department store. Unfortunately, the people of the world are not for sale.

Subhas Chandra, Psychologist, Fiji

There would be international commitment to work for the welfare and advancement of the planet earth.

Haji Mustafa Bin Abu Bakar, Director, Brunei Darussalam

"Friends for Life", Gemma Soler Raspau, Age 15, Spain

Formulae for reviving cities are as different as the origins of the cities themselves. The problems beleaguering our cities, particularly our inner city areas, are also different depending on the city you are dealing with. What I feel will trigger the renaissance and rejuvenation of these once proud cities will be opportunities afforded by two things:

1. The enterprise and endeavour of ordinary people, and
2. The recycling and reusing of once proud buildings for new uses.

In both aspects, the architectural profession has to play a leading role. By tapping the resources of ordinary people, many of whom are unemployed in these areas, decaying inner cities can rebuild their self respect. It is also important for city politicians to realize the limitation of their power. They are not in control of the market forces. If they have the interests of their city at heart - which obviously they do - they can trigger interest by those who can eventually pay the bills. Make the town a practical place to live in and then it will be easy to attract good personnel and good staff and persuade top managers and entrepreneurs to move in with all their expertise and skills.

The architect's role is to respond to this rather unique challenge of creating jobs. The locals must benefit from the new wealth creation. They must be the labour force. Enthusiasm can be imported into areas of destitution and dereliction but those who have suffered from the latter have to be the first beneficiaries of this imported energy, because they will be the very people who can either make or break a scheme. Self interest has to be seen as a basic moving force and must be encouraged. What better way to do this than to tap the resources of human endeavour available in these areas of greatest need. The architectural profession, for its part, has the vision. The inner cities need resources of available labour and the vision of the architect - a vital combination to trigger and sustain the inner city renaissance.

Rod Hackney, Architect, UK

My vision is that politicians and decision-makers see much further than they do today when they make their decisions. They have to know that they have been chosen as trustees for the wishes of the whole of humanity. There is no more space for personal ambition for power - it is unmodern - it is out! We have to serve the world, our earth and ourselves.

Christina Oden, Body Therapist, Sweden

All governments must respect and use the principles within their own country firstly and secondly with other nations.

Mohamed Soliman, Scientist, Syria

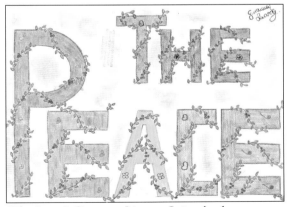
"The Peace", Giovanna Lacorty, Switzerland

"Transformation of World by Peace", Marilda Mallet, Brazil

National governments and non-governmental organizations within countries should have, as a high priority, working for peace with justice in the world, and particularly in the region where they are located. This will necessitate transcending historical allegiances and military ties in order to assert the desirability of peacefulness within and between nations, with justice and equity provided for all citizens, whatever their race, colour, creed or economic level.

Governments will not achieve this alone, but only with the "consent of the people", and this is commonly found both through democratic elections and through the work of non-governmental agencies - voluntary societies where people bind themselves together on a common basis to achieve certain agreed goals.

Archdeacon Alan Nichols, Refugee Worker, Australia

My vision of a better world is one in which the developed countries would cooperate with the oppressed peoples all over the world, and show enough goodwill to give the developing nations a chance to survive.

Fela Anikulapo-Kuti, Musician, Nigeria

It is high time now that we start labouring to be beautiful and make this world a family of nations where every nation can live with peace and security, love and cooperation as members of a family. United we can make the family of nations a living and palpable reality and each individual can contribute to its actualization through his/her own purity of thought and creativity of action.

Mahesh Kumar Upadhyaya, Vice-Chancellor, Nepal

All individuals would consider themselves as administrators of the universe and not owners. Actions would thus have this basis.

Laurence C. Ciantar, Consultant, Malta

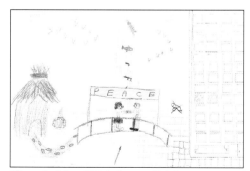
"Peace", Marc Winkelmans, Belgium

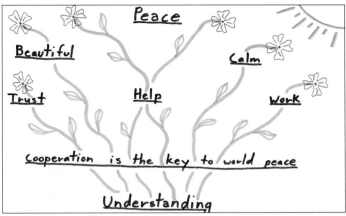

Illustrated Cinquain poem, Hiroki Yamagashi, Micronesia

Cooperation is fun
you don't have to work and run.
Cooperation is neat
which you can't beat.
Cooperation is cool
it's like swimming in a swimming pool.

Student, New Zealand

Whatever one country needs, another will provide following the principle of sharing what they have in excess and as a commitment and responsibility to other countries. Each country and culture has something unique to share and therefore there is mutually cooperative exchange at global and national levels.

Roundtable Group, Philippines

To create an ideal society, it is essential to establish an advanced social system that will respect the public as the people become the master of their nation and community and furthermore, on this foundation, there must be a combined effort or cooperation to transform the people and their activity to rebuild the nation and society. And it is an honourable and glorious duty for progressive human beings and enlightened people to participate in this activity to create a new world that will fulfil the people's interests and rights to peace, and a prosperous future.

Kang ung bin, Director, Democratic People's Republic of Korea

I would like to see a commitment by all governments and peoples throughout the world that they would all work towards a world where there are no more conflicts or wars, no more nuclear weapons and where the environment would be protected.

Sela Molisa, Minister, Vanuatu

I say that for the achievement of this better world the people in it should put their heads together and try to find a way because where there is a will there is a way.

Godfrey Kayembe, Student, Zambia

Our hope for peace is mirrored on the happy faces of children. They lead us to hammer our swords into ploughs and our spears into pruning knives. The streets of the world will again be full of boys and girls playing and shouting: "We have Peace!" Peace is the fruit of justice and integrity.

Cardinal Paulo Evaristo Arns, Archbishop of Sao Paulo, Brazil

Amenah Abu-Safean, Age 14, Jordan

You cannot rely on one person to change situations. It is a question of a lot of people getting together, either people who are themselves in the same situation or people who feel compassion or empathy with the situation of those people. Then when they get together we have political action which is a uniquely human characteristic. So much so that the political aspect of a person's life is what makes a person a person, a human a human. In fact politics is a Greek word; it stems from the word "polis" which, in modern Greek too, means "city" and "getting together". Its etymology has to do with the verb that means to get close to each other, to approach each other, getting together on a rational basis in which we understand each other and what we are doing. This is politics in the human sense. Animals are in herds or groups but they do not have the rational discourse and rational understanding that makes humans getting together distinctly human and therefore political. We cannot escape from our political character - we cannot hide in our individual world and forget what is going on outside. What is happening outside our house is something that affects our house, it affects our being, our souls because humans are inherently, from the beginning, political. They are meant, they are bound, they are condemned if you want, to live together with other humans and interact. I say condemned only to show the inescapability of the situation because for me it is not a condemnation, it is a blessing. I said that only to express that it is not up to us, we cannot decide to be otherwise - that is the inescapability of the situation.

Dimitris Moschopoulos, Diplomat, Greece

Peace is a way of living not just the end of war. If all people were to have a greater sense of love and tolerance we could achieve a better world in which everyone can live in peace and harmony. We need to see peace in a more moral way in which we think of peace not just as the end of war or armaments but rather as a spiritual concept which everyone can practise in terms of self-transformation. We must understand the purpose of life on earth and the aim of human existence.

William Koffi Adjoyi, International Civil Servant, Togo

The public awareness that there is now was not there twenty years ago. The world may shout but people change at their own pace. In Eastern Europe things are happening but for them to be the really democratic people we dream of will take time - it will not happen overnight. How can you change your mind overnight when you don't even know what thinking democratically means? It involves progressive thinking. Change is like a child growing up, you take each step. If you were born where everything was already in place you wouldn't realize what it takes to change, grow and accept. Laws might change overnight but it takes time for those laws to achieve their intentions. It takes time for people to appreciate the intention of the law and for the law to take effect in people's lives.

Rose Olende, Lawyer/Diplomat, Kenya

An innovative system to make a better world could be considered the modern non-violent movement of masses that can, in a peaceful way, change an oppressive totalitarian system into a system of pluralistic democracy. It happened in Poland in 10 years, in Hungary within 10 months, in East Germany within 10 weeks, in Czechoslovakia within 10 days and Romania within 10 hours, unfortunately with casualities.

The most powerful way in which to reach better understanding among people throughout the world would be considered the free movement of ideas and people across boundaries/frontiers.

"Friendship", Beata Dymarska, Age 17, Poland

Mihalik Josef, Professor, Slovakia

At the time of making decisions, it is convenient to use the system of consensus, making sure that the goals of the members coincide, and that the spirit of unanimity reigns in the community so that all objections be discussed and overcome. It should be kept in mind that if minorities are oppressed by majorities, there cannot be harmony in the community. Moreover, if it is true that this mechanism can slow down the process of making decisions, it guarantees that all the members will make their best efforts to cooperate once a decision is made.

Gabriel Awad, Engineer, Colombia

Despite the obvious perils the world faces in terms of weaponry, poverty and population, the remedy is in our hands. What we need is the political will to apply some of the miracles science has provided. *Robyn Williams, Broadcaster, Australia*

"Let's Live Together in Peace" – Winner of Global Cooperation "Kids of the World" Art Competition, organized by Ansett Airlines, Club Mediterranee and the UN Pavilion at Expo '88. Kylie Coffey, Australia

I propose the nomination of "sages" who would be the guarantors of authenticity, wisdom, peace, harmony and humanitarianism and to whom the governing leaders would be subjected for main line decisions. The ideal would eventually be not to have frontiers between nations and that each one of us would have started his internal transformation towards peace, respect and wisdom in relation to the self and those around us, as demonstrated by those who would be nominated.

Jean-Marie Vivien, Post Office Worker, France

It gives me a great pleasure to imagine the world that I am very willing to live in for the few days of my remaining life on this planet.

My people nearby in the west bank suffering from the occupation; the farmers in my village waiting with their eyes to the sky for the rain to grow their crops. My mother is looking to the face of my ill father who seems that he is carrying a heavy load.

In this disastrous situation my mind was going on thinking of a better world that everybody will be happy in. I imagine the world that I like to live in. A world without nuclear and atomic weapons, without poverty, wars, fears from ill, a world with clean environment, with sufficient food for all people, a world in which human beings cooperate to protect it for us and for our children.

Then immediately, the shouting of my infant brother for milk attracted me to my real world, a world full of difficulty and tears.

Ruba Nasser El-Omari, Student, Jordan

If we were to make sure that everybody on this earth had a chance really to have these choices to survive, to be healthy, to be knowledgeable, to have some means of ensuring a decent living then people would take care of themselves. If you enable people to take care of themselves, different values and norms emerge. If people really had a better chance to say what they want, to do what they want, the world would look quite different. All the scepticism about whether people make the right choices is because we present people with the wrong world. You cannot blame people for smoking their lives away when at the same time they are presented with an advertisement showing that smoking is cool and healthy.

Basically we have the wealth and the income to ensure a decent life for all. We must urge political leaders in developing countries to do as much as they can with their existing resources, showing that they are serious about development so that they can win more trust from their development partners. For their part, the developed countries should have a more enlightened attitude and see that in the longer term opportunities cannot be concentrated in one place and must be voluntarily shared in order to avoid endangering their own achievement.

Inge Kaul, International Civil Servant, Germany

I'm thinking already what profession I'll choose - I want to be a lawyer and to do my best for our government.

Marina Buntina, Pupil, Russia

From the Global Cooperation Art Contest "My Idea of a Better World", Hong Kong,
Wei-Yuan Lo, Age 16, Hong Kong

Winner of consolation prize in the Global Cooperation Art Contest, "My Idea of a Better World", Hong Kong, Chan Wing Yan, Age 14, Hong Kong

In a Better World:

Science serves humanity and appropriate technology is applied to ensure sustainable development and enhance the quality of life.

科学为人类服务,应用适当的科技来保证持续的发展并促进生活质量。

Наука и техника служат человеку, обеспечивают устойчивое развитие и улучшают качетво жизни.

La science est au service de l'humanité, et la technologie appropriée sert à assurer un développement durable et une meilleure qualité de vie.

يخدم العلم الانسانية ، وتطبق التكنولوجية المناسبة لتأمين
التطور المستمر وتعزيز قيمة الحياة .

La ciencia está al servicio de la humanidad, y se utiliza la tecnología apropiada para lograr un desarrollo sostenible y mejorar la calidad de vida.

11 SCIENCE AND THE QUALITY OF LIFE

The new science must be human-centred. This needs a new thinking in interpreting the subject and the aims of science.

J. Horvath, Philosopher, Hungary

The real progress of science and technology should be focused to realize our life in harmony with the Globe.

Toshimichi Iiyama, Geologist, Japan

In our better world, science will have the purpose of bringing benefit to humanity and to nature. Scientists will aim to elevate the living standards of humanity and will never allow their discoveries and inventions to be used for any negative purpose. Science will neither try to possess nor to conquer the natural laws, but it will know them, it will respect them, and it will function within their framework.

Roundtable Group, Greece

The money spent on creating machines to kill people should be used to make them live. Therefore technology should be used very carefully to avoid destruction of man and environment.

Gulseren Gunce, Psychiatrist, Turkey

My vision is of a world where science is used to protect, not destroy the environment.

Nicole Razafindrakoto, Researcher, Madagascar

Developed countries should have the awareness that all technology should be transferable, subject to consideration of its social security implications.

Maria Teresa Forero de Saade, Minister, Colombia

The world is threatened to be divided into a world possessing modern technology and a world lacking it. We are in a period which is going to witness wide jumps in science which is going to change the outlook of the world. The guaranteed transfer of modern technology and the freedom to deal with it and the work of alleviating the poor ensures the progress of international society as a whole.

Mohamed Ganem El Ramihi, Kuwait

"Technology is the way", Sotonye Afiesimama, Nigeria

"Science is for Construction not Destruction", Divya Sharma, India

The spendings on science at present are very meagre. They must be increased about 5-fold to engineer visible progress. The rich and developed countries should help the poor countries generously, financially as well as through their scientific community, to build their science base.

The level of science education in the poor countries must be raised through the efforts of local governments supported by rich nations and international agencies.

If, through such measures, the gap in science and technology between the rich and poor nations is narrowed, the poor nations will no longer remain poor and most of the misery seen in those lands can vanish.

Abdus Salam, Physicist, Italy

In our better world, research has a sound ethical foundation, a holistic orientation and is focused on humanitarian issues, with the aim of improving the quality of life whilst respecting ecological balances. Different scientific groups share their ideas through a network and a centralized research entity. Science helps to raise consciousness and remind people of what they are and where they come from. Financial support for research is provided by neutral, independent sources.

Roundtable Group, Switzerland

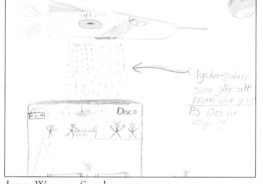

Jonas Wangso, Sweden

In my ideal world, the role of a scientist would be that of a sage, conscious of his/her limits, humble and modest in front of the immensity of the universe's phenomena, which have still to be discovered and understood, and whose only aim would be to develop science in order to help humanity.

Nicole Scotto di Carlo, Research Director, France

The mobilization of human capacity through a new consciousness of belonging (translated into a determined political will, using the constructive potential of technology, and its new developments and the enormous economic resources used today for armaments) is certainly able to generate the transition towards a higher state of civilization, towards the achievement of a level of humanity never known of before.

Gilberto Carlos Gallopin, Ecologist, Argentina

"My Ideal World", Trudy Le Bas, Age 12, UK

The cars would be small and run on water, Trudy Le Bas.

"Students for World Peace", Judy Fraley with art students on "Global Mind Change" course, USA

The first asset to be secured in the vision of a global future as finally established by the principles of sustainable development is that of a better quality life where all enjoy equal rights for clean air to breathe, pure water to drink and wholesome food for essential nourishment and survival. Working towards that end, the world of the future has to establish mandatory environmental impact assessment, an emphasis on clean technologies (eventually depending on the use of renewable energy sources, the clean sources of nature), optimising the use of natural resources, proper treatment and recycling of most (if not all) waste products and international cooperation.

El-Mohamady Eid, Environmentalist, Egypt

There are areas where there may be new forms of transport. For instance, I can imagine there will be places with automatic rolling platforms that will take you along streets, or longer trips, without even paying. Or there may be things like private or separate flying capabilities using gadgets attached to you.

M. Dvir, Executive Vice-President, Israel

My vision is that science will turn its attention to understanding that deepest of all questions: What are the processes in Nature which produce our human ability to be conscious, to think, to believe, to chose value systems. The current scientific wisdom, 'A cosmic accident', is not the correct answer. Only when this is done will humanity understand itself well enough to begin to reason together from a common basis. Not that people will ever totally agree but at least we need to reason from knowledge of the same basic principles.

Edgar Mitchell, Astronaut, USA

My own personal vision would be to see a world in which all scientific researchers, technological advances, exploration of space (both inner and outer) and social science researches including paranormal researches would be directed to achieve, in accelerated fashion, the peoples' vision.

Laike Mariam Asfaw, Seismologist, Ethiopia

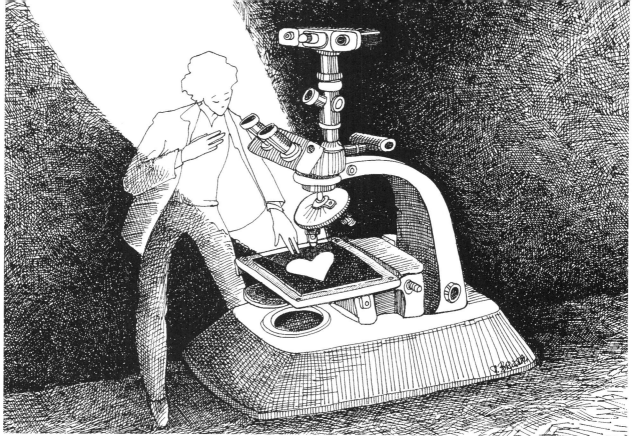

Murielle Briot, Belgium

How about a global network to tap solar energy in tropical regions and transfer it around the world to provide electricity to those who need it?

Based on the application of direct solar and associated "renewable" energies as a major source (gradually replacing fossil and nuclear), a strategy must be evolved into global, as well as regional and local planning, for a supply and distribution system to realize the potential capacity of solar energy effectively and economically.

Such a strategy may lead to a global girdle of electrical power generating units in the tropical regions. These units will run on energy from the sun obtained by using concentrating collectors globally around the clock. Such a global solar network becomes economically feasible because only the initial capital costs are involved without recurring "fuel" costs.

Such one-mega watt units are economic, can be set up and linked up to form a grid in a district, then to a region and can be extended all over the world. It needs no expert to say that solar energy is almost completely free from pollution and that it presents very low risks of lethal or fatal hazard situations.

Neil J. Shendge, Scientist, UK

Technology is used in our daily life. The people will be the creators of technology. Technology will not be in the hands of only a few. Everyone will have technological 'know-how'. Technology and freedom should go together.

Roundtable Group, Mexico

Science is about knowledge - it is derived from the Latin word for knowledge "scientia". Technology - by my definition - is about solving problems in a specified time and place. Technology is much older than science.

Technology was born, in my view, the day a young neanderthal man came to the edge of a deep gorge in the earth and looked across and saw on the other edge a neanderthal maid. They looked at the gorge and then at each other again and said "how?" Their first child could have been named "Technology".

It is only in the last fifty years that mankind has started using science as a basis for the creation of technology. To my mind, the transition took place just about when the transistor was developed - around 1947. For all the millennia before mankind was developing technology to satisfy his needs and science followed later to explain the phenomena that were already being utilized.

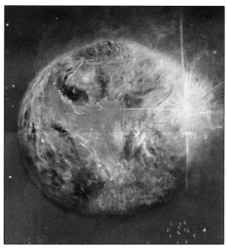

"Rebirth of the World",
Marie Binder, France

Technology arises in response to a human need i.e. to solve a problem. I cannot postulate a better world which appears suddenly overnight so I have to consider what changes can take place in today's world to give rise to my better world. Fortunately for me, there are already many signs that such changes are possible.

Since the time of the neanderthal boy and girl, mankind has used his technological creativity to take control of his environment. Technological developments in this century alone have placed in the hands of ordinary individuals a capability to exercise control over their lives and their environment, which was not previously enjoyed even by absolute monarchs. What we are finding, however, and with increasing urgency, is that we have developed our technological solutions in a very piecemeal fashion and without recognition of the interlocking relationships which make up the closed bio-system we inhabit.

In my better world I see integration of technology such that human needs are satisfied by means which take a holistic approach to the terrestrial bio-system i.e. our technology would no longer be piecemeal solutions - specific to the time and place of need - but will be integrated technology recognizing the interdependent nature of all life - and especially human life. This implies a value system which upholds the fundamental fact of interdependence.

Hollis Charles, Engineer,
Trinidad & Tobago

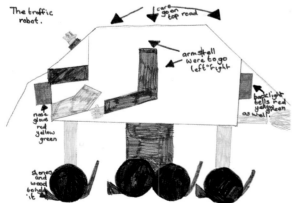

"The Traffic Robot", Coston School, UK

Since the first flint tool, new systems and artifacts have changed those who used them permanently and irreversibly. In the main, the process by which innovation comes about is one in which concepts or artifacts are brought together in a novel way. When this occurs, the result tends to be more than the sum of the parts. For this reason, the social effects of innovation have, in general, been unexpected and unforeseen. These effects have triggered other changes, generating a kind of ripple effect.

In the main, society has been incapable of second-guessing or controlling these effects of change, the end-product of which has serendipitously acted for good or ill. Throughout history, the social effects of change have been tightly linked to surges in the ability to transmit and receive information. The greater that ability, the faster the rate of change and the more profound and widespread its effect. Writing, hieroglyphics, print, telecommunication and data-processing have each contributed to major advances in mankind's ability to manufacture new knowledge and to implement it in the form of technology. The result has been to induce a rate of change in the modern world with which most ordinary people find it impossible to keep up. It is said that new-model replacement happens so quickly these days that if you understand how an artifact works, the artifact must already be obsolete.

Unfortunately, since Descartes' exposition of the mechanics of reductionism, which greatly accelerated the rate at which science was able to innovate, the means to do so has become increasingly specialized and esoteric. More and more is known about less and less. This process isolates innovators from the rest of the community and makes even more difficult any attempt to understand their work.

At root in all this is the rationalist tradition of so-called "free enquiry". This, in spite of the fact that there is no such thing. Innovation and discovery have never been entirely free, but rather socially sourced, whether by shaman, priest-king, monarch, ideology or Chief Executive Officer. The investigation which produces innovation has always been at the behest of some institution or other and has almost never been directed at the demise of that institution, but to enhance the chances of its survival.

The fact that, on occasion, innovation has the opposite effect on the institution has almost always been accidental. The Copernican search, on behalf of the Catholic Church, for a system that would improve the calculation of the date of Easter and which led to the heliocentric system and ultimately to the rise of Protestantism was a classic case in point.

Between scientific specialization, market dynamics and institutionalism, then, the origin or trigger of innovation has almost always been guarded from public gaze. However, if the potential social effects of innovation in the coming convergence of data-processing with

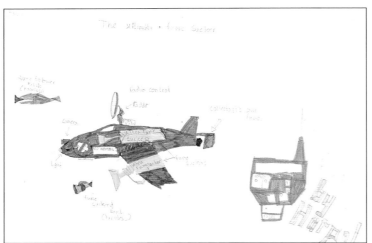

"The Ultimate Fume Suckers", Harpal, Coston School, UK

"The Life and Light of Science", Val Riabovol, Russia

telecommunications are not to have the same unexpected and widely disruptive effects on society (representing as they will the greatest force for change perhaps in history) it is urgently necessary that protective action be taken as soon as possible.

At every level, efforts must be directed at improving the educational standards of the population at large. Only an informed electorate can make informed decisions about public issues such as the direction of scientific and technological research. The mechanism of innovation must eventually be placed in the public arena. Science and technology are so pervasive that their increasingly-powerful effects can no longer be regarded as a matter solely of the freedom of individual self-expression.

Education is the prime tool through which to enfranchise the public. Knowledge is power and with technologies like hypermedia we now have the means for the first time to place knowledge in the hands of the many instead of the few who have guided social development so far. If the massive creative potential of the four billion under-educated brains on the planet can be released in this way, then participatory democracy becomes a practical possibility.

These circumstances are unlikely to come about through direct action on the part of the individual. Rather they should come at the behest of present-day governments, acting to encourage by whatever means those organizations and industries which have the means and the expertise to disseminate the necessary technologies, if only as an expression of enlightened self-interest.

The first open, global communications network may soon exist. It can be used to enhance and centralize the power of the few as never before. Or it can offer the opportunity for the advent of the first true cultural and political pluralism in history, through which global society will be able for the first time, to shape its own, collective destiny.

James Burke, Journalist and Writer, UK

Trudie Elizabeth Roffey, UK

In a Better World:

All people enjoy freedom of expression, movement and belief while respecting the liberties and rights of others.

人人都享受言论、行动和信仰自由，并同时尊重他人的自
由与权利。

Человеку обеспечена свобода слова, передвижения и
вероисповедания, и он уважает свободы и права других.

Chacun jouit de la liberté d'expression, de déplacement et d'opinion,
tout en respectant les libertés et les droits d'autrui.

١٢. يتمتع الناس جميعاً، بحرية التعبير، والتنقل، والمعتقد
بينما يحترمون حريات وحقوق الآخرين.

Todas las personas gozan de libertad de expresión, movimiento y credo,
al tiempo que respetan las libertades y los derechos de los demás.

12 FREEDOM AND RESPONSIBILITY

There should be freedom of giving and sharing amongst all human beings regardless of culture, educational background, race and religion.
Lawrence Foanaota, Museum Director, Solomon Islands

All people are free - in all aspects. All nations (large and small) are free. Every nation lives in its land and uses its language. Borders between countries are symbolic.
Aija Zhilewitch, Medical Practitioner, Latvia

A world in which everyone is free to speak their mind and elect the government of their choice; a world which is free from militarism, racism and social and economic injustice.
Michael Macklin, Senator, Australia

I'd like to have peace and freedom in the world in the near future; also equality with other countries. I must be free to speak without fear.
Thushara Fernando, Flying Officer, Sri Lanka

I believe that it is absolutely important to respect the opinions and ideas of others.
Edgar Rodas Andrade, Surgeon, Ecuador

In a better world, people respect each others' decisions and have the freedom to do what they want for the good of the community they live in.
Claire G. Lazaro, Sales Executive, Philippines

All human society would be based on principles of democracy, freedom and tolerance of belief.
A. K. Agbodjan, Technician, Togo

Free movement and choice of people across countries.
Creative Group, France

I think people should be free to move anywhere or any place. People should not be treated as robots and should not be restricted to go to any area.
Ganess Rama, Student, South Africa

"Birth of Light", Christian Dasen, Switzerland

A world without boundaries in which we travel without passports and in which visas are not needed.
Narain Bholanath, Surveyor, Suriname

Through peace and faith, freedom is born.
Eeyad, Student, Jordan

Enrique Santamaria, Age 17, Spain

Each human being should be able to move freely on this earth without having to go through these interminable procedures for a visa.
J. A. Rakotoarisoa, Museum Director, Madagascar

Different ideas and beliefs, whether they be ideological, religious or other, should be allowed to bloom and compete and people should not be persecuted for the ideas they espouse or views and beliefs that they uphold. A better world is not one where there is uniformity or unanimity of opinions but one in which a plurality of views is tolerated and one that is flexible enough to accommodate conflicting ones.
Daniel Haile, Lawyer, Ethiopia

Help people to actualize themselves through more freedom which in itself would lead them to be more responsible of themselves and others.
Kianoosh Hashemian, Psychologist, Iran

The United Nations should implement a new system which offers to people the means to express themselves freely.
Odette Roy Fombrun, Writer, Haiti

I would like to see a world without borders, where people of all races are found living harmoniously in every region.
Chinniah Sathyanoorthy, Teacher, Singapore

Every individual should enjoy freedom of worship.
Syed Zainal Adidin Bin S.A.M. Jamalullail (Datuk), Secretary-General, Malaysia

I will want to have a world where God is the centre of all life. There should be freedom of religion and worship in harmony with the existing laws of the country.
Margaret Yalley, Rev. Minister, Ghana

I would like to include the idea of God and the principle of religious freedom. The rights and duties of the individual conscience should not be overlooked.
Nicholas J. Cauchi, Roman Catholic Bishop, Malta

"Flying Bird",
Maria Lourdes T. Lapa, Philippines

Freedom is the ability to achieve to the fullest, the God-given work of pursuing life. This freedom is for every creature the right and the opportunity to experience the fullness of its being. This freedom is a wonderful gift. To pursue my own life fully requires of me to acknowledge the freedom you have to do the same. Living my life to the fullest is loving God, myself, and everyone and everything which God has made. Loving them is longing for them, as I do for myself, the experience of the fullness of their being.

That being is physical, social, intellectual, spiritual. Thus, it is incumbent upon me and all of us to work to eliminate poverty, famine, disease, oppression, violence, ignorance, fear and all that promotes death and not life; to promote health, knowledge, justice and peace for all.

We have the freedom to contemplate a world such as this, and we have the freedom to bring it about.

Lloyd S. Casson, Canon, Episcopal Church, USA

Thomas E., Lasse Pernille, Line M., Age 9, Hedehusene School, Denmark

The so-called freedom most relevant to the peasants in China is freedom from starvation, freedom from lack of the essential needs. Then if you are ill you will have access to a doctor, if you work you will be secure in knowing that your harvest will be good. And if you want your children to go to elementary school or junior high school then you can send them there. Another freedom, which perhaps they don't talk about so much, is freedom from hard labour - they work so hard, harder than animals. They want to find a new way.

Pat Tung, China

In my future better world I see a world where there is respect for all the opinions of others and respect for their freedom to express themselves in any way they want as well as the systematic boycott of any form of dictatorial or totalitarian regime in this planet of ours.

Paquito D'Rivera, Musician, Cuba

I will respect each person's right of choice. I will recognise the innate dignity of every individual with whom I come into contact by listening. Harness positive energy for the good of those around me and myself. Have fun and never stop discovering.

Rohini Delilkhan, Hotelier, Hong Kong

Every individual would have the right to culture and faith without jeopardizing the interest of others.

Costantinos Berhe, President, Ethiopia

There would be responsibility of every human being in liberty for each human being of a people that does not have access to liberty and dignity.

Georgeta Praisler, Ph.D., Romania

Suspended between heaven and earth I conquered freedom. The freedom of heart of a young boy who once grown up ensured being always free by choosing God's freedom.

Unknown, Italy

A VISION AND A TASK CAN CHANGE THE WORLD

"Power of Innocence", Marie Binder, France.

Formulating a clear and positive vision of a better world was a significant aspect of participating in the Global Cooperation project but just as important as any vision is the plan of action to realize it. Project participants were encouraged to develop action plans that went at least some way towards making their vision a reality and in many cases saw the necessity of cooperating with others to do so. This Chapter provides an overview of some of these plans and actions and the ways in which people were able to work together with others towards a common goal.

Most of the project's diverse activities were planned and implemented locally, and independently of other events, but all had at least one thing in common - they provided people with an often longed-for opportunity to offer something to the world. Participants could see that they were not alone in their endeavours, that there were other people - all over the world - who shared their concerns and aspirations. In this way the activities themselves, no matter how unique or inspiring they may have been, became almost secondary to the fact that people came away from them feeling in some way enriched, that they had heard the sound of a forgotten chord within themselves. No matter what it was they had done, people had become involved, with their hearts, minds and bodies, and felt that this could make a difference…

In the past few years we've seen on a world scale what can be achieved through cooperation and yet at the same time have been reminded of how far we have to go.

On the optimistic side we've seen the members of the United Nations and the Secretary-General working as never before to help bring about and keep peace in conflict-ridden lands. We've seen that the shadow of a nuclear holocaust seems to be moving further and further away. Major nations and national leaders have woken up to the fearful degradation of the environment for which every one of us must accept a share of the blame. In peoples' minds, as the vision shows us, green items are now firmly on the agenda. It's become possible to see the sort of world the Global Vision describes for us.

Yet in every continent, in every community and in every family we are also faced by monumental problems. Naturally these problems assume different dimensions according to our geography, our environment, and our understanding of global issues but whatever the problems may be, they often look not just daunting but insoluble. The reactions which arise in most people are: "How can I and my family, my friends and workmates bring about disarmament, environmental protection, a fairer distribution of resources, justice and tolerance - even if I understand what these terms mean? I don't know how to go about it and feel helpless. Anyhow there are organizations of experts at a community, national and international level set up to find solutions. Isn't it best to leave these problems to the Council or City Authorities, the Government and the United Nations? Let them get on with it, there is nothing we as individuals can do to create a better world - or for that matter a better town or village. Best left to the experts."

Children playing for a better world at Araguari Coffee Fair, Brazil.
(Calimerio Resende Avila, Brazil)

Wrong, quite wrong. We all suffer more from lack of motivation, of human energy and commitment than from lack of expertise.

Participants in the Global Cooperation project were asked to contribute their ideas and visions of a better world using their inherent potential as human beings before professional qualifications. But how can we tackle the mountains of problems ahead without a vision of the other side, without a plan, or even a sense of direction? We need to know where we are going and how we can cooperate to get there. It is easy to become mesmerized by the size of problems which confront us daily. We need to cast our eyes upward and evolve a vision of the sort of world we would like to live in.

For example, there are many millions of people facing starvation in Africa and elsewhere. Appeals are made on television and radio. But what is our vision? It is certainly not of soup kitchens, and food queues, creating dependency and indignity. If we have a vision of a world which uses its resources to grow enough food for all, without wastage, corruption or incompetence, it helps us to work on the means of achieving these long term objectives.

As we think, talk and create our vision together the concepts come thick and fast. Global Cooperation asked individuals, as well as groups: "What do you want to see in your better world?" People answered: "Enough good food and clean water; freedom to share it; adequate housing, education and health care; social, economic and political justice; freedom to say what we want; an atmosphere of love, trust, friendship and mutual respect". The vision gradually became clearer.

Of course there are the self-seekers and those who want power for its own sake, but fundamentally most people want the same things for themselves and society: that is the evidence of this project as illustrated by the twelve point Global Vision Statement with its supporting visions from over 120 countries. Whether it is a group of students, a room of elderly people, children in a village school, professionals at an international seminar, shoe-shine boys in Brazil, natives of an Indian village, working mothers from urban slums, a Head of State or the Head of a U.N. Agency - whoever, whenever, wherever - they want the same.

The second challenge is to turn the vision into reality. Few, if any, solutions are achieved without individual commitment and a sense of responsibility. We must remember that together with rights go responsibilities. Such a sense of universal responsibility for one another takes time - and even when achieved is inadequate unless there is cooperation between individuals, groups and communities.

If we really are - at any level - to turn vision into reality, we need to practise the art of cooperation and of living together as good neighbours as set out in the preamble to the United Nations Charter signed in 1945. There is not much that can be achieved by individuals working on their own; some fame and popularity perhaps, but it is short lived. How often have we heard politicians in different countries and from different parties pontificating about how they hope to achieve their particular objective. I am not arguing that there is no place for competition; but nothing lasting or valuable can be achieved without effective cooperation. Of that I am sure.

Common goals must emerge from varying hopes, needs and aspirations, however long it takes. Failure to reach agreement is not acceptable. Individual and collective responsibility is needed not only to turn the vision into reality but to maintain the momentum of cooperation.

So, now is the time to call on the will and clear vision of the people. Our actions must be based on the shared vision of a better world and on human and moral values. The views and voice of the people must be heard. It is the people of the world who by their activities, participation and cooperation can change this beautiful but sometimes sad world in which we live. It takes great effort and sometimes sacrifice but unless we get ourselves right we have little hope of getting the world right.

The Rt. Hon. Lord Ennals of Norwich, PC, UK
Co-Chairman, International Advisory Commitee,
Global Cooperation for a Better World

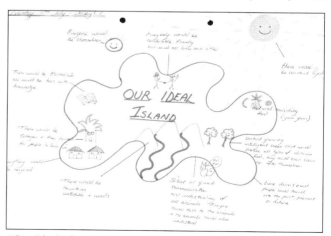

"Our Ideal Island", Creative Group, Channel Islands, UK

Section 1 - Plans and Actions

Individual and creative group participants were asked to consider action plans in relation to the broad categories of better self, better relationships or better world and examples of each of these are given below.

Global Cooperation artwork, India.

I. Self

The present world conditions are due to individual and collective attitudes and actions of human beings. And all attitudes and actions, political, economic, social, etc., have their origin in thoughts, ideas or beliefs of men and women. So in order to translate the vision into action, we have first to transform our thoughts which in turn will change our attitudes, outlook and behaviour and, finally, the world conditions. The following are suggested as some principles of behaviour which we can use as matrices of our actions in order to change the Vision into a Better World.

We may resolve to put into action the following principles:

1. We will be fair, honest, upright and sincere in our work or profession and our actions will match our words and promises.

2. Our dealings with others will be free from prejudice, rancour, vain-glory and exploitation, social, economic, sexual, racial or of any kind.

3. The guiding principle for all our actions will be universal love, sympathy, consideration, cooperation and maintenance of peace or "To be good and to do good".

4. We will not be slaves to sensual pleasures, passions or to animal urges nor will we be mad about power and position, nor will we ever adopt unfair means to gain a higher place and never will we use our power or position to harm or injure anyone.

5. We will solve our disputes through dialogue, discussions, negotiation, conciliation, arbitration or through legal processes, and will not resort to verbal or physical violence or any form of physical or mental torture.

6. We will share our responsibility in making the world an abode of health, wealth, happiness, holiness, freedom, and fraternal feelings and, in this, we will make the utmost effort and observe the utmost caution not to spoil or pollute our environment and ecological balance, or our relationship with other living beings, or even our mind and conscience.

7.   We will have an attitude of love, help and cooperation.

8.   We will spend some time daily in introspection, meditation, silence and study for our spiritual and moral development.

9.   We will look on the good qualities of others and keep stabilised in our own original, peaceful and divine nature and look on all as beloved brother souls, with God as our most beloved Mother-Father.

Jagdish Chander Hassija, Spokesperson,
Brahma Kumaris World Spiritual University, India

Ten commandments for a Better World:

I.   Wash yourself thoroughly, so that your cleanliness shines.

II.   Forget and forgive.

III. Open your ears and listen to people, then the world will be a lot more beautiful and easier.

IV.   Smile, smile and smile - it is good for your health. Say hello to others. Even the biggest sulker will have to smile back one day.

V.   Turn off television now and then. And let's plant a tree or let us visit somebody. Somebody who is alone.

VI.   Start within your own heart. And continue. Is your own family OK? And your children? Teach them what is good. Teach them from that very young age. Teach them to share with others, and play with others.

VII. What is the difference between white and black? Between yellow and brown? We see it but they are "people". Just think: the colour, the clothes, do not matter. What's within matters. Everybody has a heart.

VIII. The people who are addicted and the ill have been going through a lot of suffering. Help them, do not reject them. Little by little they'll become people with their own heart.

IX.   Learn to love the flowers, the animals and the people. If everybody loved each other a little bit, the world would be so nice.

X.   If all the rich gave a little of their wealth to the poor, that would already be a good step towards a better world.

Lutgard Peeters, Mother, Belgium

The needs and aspirations of body, mind and spirit can no longer be addressed separately. Because we recognize more and more the integrity of human persons in all their complexity, those with a capacity to inspire and lead can no longer stand apart. A common language needs to be developed and made known with all the power of the media of communication. For some years now there has been collaboration between medicine and religion. We should now extend the bridge-building to include politics, science and spirituality. Before transformation makes much headway, I suggest that we all have to examine our consciences, both as individuals and as whole societies. Do we like what we find? Have we the courage to recognize the dark side of our own personality and the major imperfections of our society? Pride, selfishness, greed, anger, hate, lies, murder and lust all exist and we are degraded when we succumb to them. We are called to know ourselves and to take responsibility, first for our own behaviour and then, as far as we can for the conduct of our families, workplaces, local, national and international communities. This is a daunting task, but I believe it to be equally and possibly more important than the overcoming of global pollution and the evolution of a sustainable economy and leadership.

Lord Hylton, UK

A health plan which encompasses physical, mental and spiritual states may be worked out soon after birth and act as a guide for the parent. Part of the individual's responsibility to the community is to attend regular checkups to monitor the progress of the individual. Trained personal counsellors will work with the individual to help ensure that physical, mental and spiritual personal health goals are maintained.

Stephen Gould, Australia

Marissa Jacobs on the unicorn she made for "Without You it's Just a Dream", a Global Cooperation dedicated performance at the Edinburgh Fringe Festival, Scotland. (Nigel Sutton, UK)

The Government of Trinidad & Tobago is a signatory to the World Health Organization Resolution of Alma Ata and so is committed to the goal "Health for all by the year 2000". However, while actively promoting the philosophy of healthy life-styles, the Ministry of Health had not been able to undertake a more positive role in the promotion of physical fitness as an essential component of primary health care. I was actively involved in Global Cooperation for a Better World and this helped start a natural flow of thoughts and events which resulted in "Health & Fitness 1990". In our country, cancer, heart disease, cerebro-vascular disease and diabetes account for over sixty percent of mortality and ill-health. These diseases are preventable and controllable to a large extent through the recognition and avoidance or reduction of the major high risk factors. These include high cholesterol levels, smoking, alcohol and substance abuse, stress and exposure to exogenous chemicals.

Recognizing the long term effect of good health on the nation, the Chief Medical Officer of the Ministry of Health fully supported the principles and objectives of the proposed programme. He advised that a successful programme would impact significantly not only on the demand for institutional health care but also on the general economy. This is because improvement of the overall well-being of the citizen is inevitably reflected in greater productivity.

The programme was very simple and straightforward. We recommended simple disciplines - such as walking, jogging, cycling, hiking, swimming and skipping and other exercises that can be done by almost every individual. People normally walk or jog in the parks. Then we introduced stations every fifty meters so that you can stop at a station and, in addition to your walking or jogging, do push-ups or sit-ups as you desire.

It was left up to the individual to increase the repetitions. In this way it is a challenge to the individual to compete against himself/herself. Only you can improve your fitness and your health.

Ken Butcher, Manager, Trinidad & Tobago

If every individual starts to improve himself we automatically get a better world.

C.R. Jadnanansing, Civil Law Notary, Suriname

Start everyday with a couple of minutes of meditation and a strong intention to contribute in your own personal way to a better world. It helps!

Erica Terpstra, Member of Parliament, Netherlands

I do not have an idea for an amazing, ingenious invention to make the world a better place to live in, just the expression of love. I may seem like one grain of sand on the seashore, but if I make a difference in just one person's life, it would be sufficient for me.

Denise Bartelt, Student, USA

Creative group at a youth retreat outside Brussels, Belgium. (Danny Puype, Belgium)

II. Relationships

We must have respect for the people around us, for the things and for the world around us, including the environment and now space too, for we have started polluting space. They are all intertwined and we cannot isolate one from the other. For the purposes of improving the situation in the world we can go one step at a time. We cannot expect to solve all of the problems at once. We can solve one at a time. There is an obvious order of dealing with these problems - start with those that are closest to you. It is hard to envisage trying to solve society's problems when your family's problem is unsolved. In history there are many cases of great people who have made a great difference in the world and improved conditions of society. They were great revolutionaries who inevitably had to neglect their families and so the opposite happened - they solved the general problem or at least made a valid contribution towards solving it but in the process they sacrificed the immediate people, the people in their family.

The most potent weapon and the longest lasting weapon that we have for the betterment of the world is human conscience. All the other weapons, even the most potent nuclear weapon, have proved inefficient. They did not block powerful governments that did not work for their people, they did not prevent governments from collapsing. Conscience is there and all the weapons in the world cannot break that, they cannot destroy that. It is the strongest weapon we have.

Dimitris Moschopoulos, Diplomat, Greece

My primary aim was to help people and I could see that with medicine I was able to do so, but on a limited level only. The cure was effective but in most cases temporary, for after a while the patient would return not only with the same problem but with a few additional ones also. Therefore I realized that the main cause for many of the problems was psychological and the cure wasn't just medicine. Unless the psychology was treated, unless the stress, the social problem, the family problem, the economic problems were all treated, the patient would come to me with the same complaints or similar ones. So in today's society the medical profession is having to face the reality that 80-90% of ailments are psychosomatic and there is only so much that medicine can do to help patients. As a medical practitioner, I saw that with meditation I could increase my potential powers like patience, love, happiness and with these powers help my patients to help themselves.

Nirmala Kajaria, Doctor, India

Suggestions for a Global Weekly Calendar:

Monday
The day of enjoying work

Tuesday
The day when we think positively of those with a leading position and imagine them with a lot of wisdom and human feelings

Wednesday
Animals' day

Thursday
Healthy vegetation

Friday
Clean earth, water and air

Saturday
Food and good health to all people on the earth

Sunday
Happiness and closeness

Anna Thomassen, Denmark

"We would much happier if we learn to speak and listen; if we know how to get along with each other; if we didn't cheat one another; if we did things on time; if everybody could play together; if we were not so selfish; if we could trust each other."

Emma Segret Perez, Age 7, Spain

My school is a new one, and so I wanted to introduce Global Cooperation to everyone. We started by growing and planting flowers around the school. Some sponsors appreciated our keenness to such an extent that we were able to stage a National Tree Planting Ceremony. This includes shade trees, flowers, shrubs and fruit trees. We now have a working group spearheading the beautification of our school, Cherutombo Secondary School.

P.L. Musiwacho, Science Master, Zimbabwe

I was inspired to improve my relationship with my business colleagues because I wanted to make people feel cared for and noticed. I began by being more cheerful and saying good morning or good evening very sweetly. The atmosphere at work started to change and within a month my colleagues were following my example. I also gained the confidence to use my cooperative skills and lead a youth group at my local community centre.

Fabakar, Legal Secretary, Singapore

The Universal Principles for Human Dignity

1. I live and enjoy my life.
2. I take care of my physical and mental health.
3. I strive after a permanent development of my personality.
4. I consider every man and woman as equal to myself.
5. I respect every person as he or she is.
6. I'm living in harmony with my fellow man.
7. I believe in the constant improvement of human society.
8. I consider every task as a contribution to a better world.
9. I respect the physical and mental labour of others.
10. I'm responsible for maintaining our environment.
11. I use the natural resources in an economical way.
12. I live in harmony with nature.
13. All humans are my brothers.
14. I believe in our capacity to change.
15. I believe in a positive approach towards myself and others.
16. I believe in the original goodness of every soul.

Roundtable Group, Belgium

"Freedom", unknown, Belgium

My mother had 84 grandchildren at the last count and our whole extended family down to the fourth generation comes to somewhere between 480-500 family members. "Survival of the fittest" is not necessarily the criterion upon which the family bases its standards...

Coming from such a large Maori family, I quickly learned that in order to enjoy a relatively happy life the main input had to be cooperation. Discipline also plays a major part, as does responsibility, but above all is the bond of "belonging to the family". Our grandparents used to look after us as children, providing moral and spiritual sustenance, while our parents worked and provided for the whole group.

Family meetings are important as they provide an environment for introducing the younger members into the family system. Each adult member is accorded the same amount of respect, which can be difficult when decisions are made at family meetings. The younger adults, with less experience but much more enthusiasm, are often exasperated by slow decision making so arguments are rife. Some arguments are carried to such an extent that members of the family have emigrated to other countries and have washed their hands of any further connections.

Nevertheless, the pull of family connections is strong, and manifest by the planning of a family reunion in 1995; even those who emigrated have indicated their intention to attend!

The reunion will be held on the family farm south of Auckland and we are raising funds to build a large complex to accommodate the gathering. There are three architects in the family, and quite a few builders, so everyone will be pitching in over the next few years to help in the construction.

The whole exercise should be very interesting, as the family has now become very multicultural due to intermarriages with inhabitants of all continents. Maybe this scenario is ideally suited to what will become truly international cooperation. I know from my own experience that real cooperation becomes easy when there is the element of spirituality in life and a focus beyond the immediate small problems to the larger picture - whatever that picture is for you.

Jim Royal, Builder, New Zealand

Coawovi, Togo

Hong Kong youth group members implementing their action plans by cleaning up Repulse Bay Beach. (Maureen Chen, Hong Kong)

III. World

To make a better world demands most of all that we want to make a better world; that we concentrate our energy, our inventiveness and our resources on positive measures to end pollution, hunger, political and social strife wherever it threatens life or liberty. This should not be considered a matter of charity, but of duty. We should always remember that, ultimately, this planet is all that we can leave to our children.

Judi Dench, Actress, UK

My idea is to build an international museum for children where toys, games, schools, life-styles, traditions etc. of the children of the world can be shown as special exhibits. This museum has to be of an interactive nature and may serve as a venue for plays and musical performances performed by the children themselves. It should be an international centre for cultural and educational exchanges among the world's children. The museum should ideally be run under the auspices of UNESCO and should be financed by grants from donor nations and the sale of children's art or greeting cards. I feel this is one project worthy of global cooperation.

Suwa D. Fung, Undergraduate, Singapore

The need for a global research project to facilitate the shift, throughout humanity, from an egocentric mode of consciousness to one in which people can think, perceive, decide and act for the good of all. Without such a shift in consciousness, none of the goals of vision will be accomplished.

Peter Russell, Author, UK

HIV infection has become a social phenomenon which involves everyone in two ways: 1/ No one is safe and 2/ the social, ethical and political questions it raises are on everyone's mind.

Those who are not infected must 1/ take the necessary health precautions and request documentation and information which is as complete as possible, 2/ help those who are infected, who may be close to them or not, who might be children, social outcasts or simply people who are different.

Those who are infected must 1/ realize that the illness is present even when there are no symptoms and make sure that they do not infect anybody else, 2/ make a major effort in terms of their own health (good food, recommended treatment, keep abreast of medical innovations, mental exercises to avoid panic, blame and stress) and 3/ join organizations or participate in new efforts to speed up the across-the-board process of "taking charge".

Research is focusing on people, time and money: basic research,

"Operation Cooperation", a group of 15 young artists, supported by the Mayor of Redditch, UK, began implementing their vision of a better world by cleaning up a local pond. (Mandy Rogers, UK)

industrial research with unselfish motives but also with the need for companies to make a profit, primarily in terms of money. But for the time being, the most important thing is to acquire greater knowledge and find better means of treatment.

Vigilance and a spirit of enterprise must be combined to transform this struggle against disease into an adventure-crusade of modern times. Let us not forget that the modern world may well have to face other grave problems in the future and let us prepare our means of personal and collective response to prevent further losses.

François Rieger, Director of Research, CNRS, France

The degradation of the environment in the developing world is a matter of concern to all and the real hope for the future lies in funds being found to pay for the necessary human resources to supervise locally the tasks of managing problems. My wish is that every aid package from donors would carry an overhead that could be directly applied to the management costs of local environmental concerns. These funds would be used to utilize local people in professional roles normally earmarked for expatriates because of the external funding. The developing countries must be helped to be able to afford to make their part of the world a better place.

Richard Leakey, Director of Wildlife, Kenya

A lot of natural and environmental disasters occur all over the world. These include earthquakes, floods, hurricanes, volcanoes, and the dire pollution from hazardous toxic emissions of chemical factories as well as accidental atomic explosions. These disasters cause damage to all surroundings (man, plants, animals). The disaster-stricken country remains hand-tied, unable to alleviate the damage that has befallen it -

Global Cooperation Artwork, Catherine Churko, USA

even if it was expected - because of its limited financial capabilities. It has to wait for other countries to make a move towards its aid.

It is always the case that the international community unites in facing such disasters, and all countries rise to the help of the afflicted country supplying it with money, food provisions, medicine, and the necessary equipment to overcome this disaster. Hence, we have thought up this proposal which aims at establishing a unified emergency international fund for insurance against natural and environmental disasters:

* Determining a certain sum or percentage which varies according to the capabilities of developed and developing countries, to be paid by all member countries of the international community.

* This sum - which is to be paid at regular periods to be agreed upon - represents an insurance against natural and environmental disaster. The collected amount of money is to be put in an international fund under the supervision of the United Nations Organization.

* The above-mentioned fund aims at providing financial assistance to the stricken countries

Atef Mohamed Ebeid, Minister of Cabinet Affairs, Minister of Environment, Egypt

It was decided to compile a list of all the unaccompanied children under 16 years of age with no parents to care for them in our refugee camp. We look after these children by paying regular visits. We have small talks with them, telling them not to fight; to avoid drugs and the bad people who offer them; to go to school; to be good and kind to people and to keep their bodies clean and healthy.

Tran Van Hung, Bui Bich Nga, Nguyen Thi Phong, Trinh Thi Bicmhoa,
Save the Children Health Educators, Tuen Mun Vietnamese Refugee Camp, Hong Kong

I ascribe myself to this initiative of creating an International Green Cross that points to the ecological preservation of our planet.

Daniel Alvarez Gantier, Chemical Engineer, Bolivia

Form a group of 15 environmentally-conscious people, representing different disciplines and then through a campaign showing the relationship between the environment and health, it is possible to stimulate consumers to buy foods and products which do not affect the environment. We are requesting the Government that products be labelled as to their safety for the environment.

Herman van de Neut, Retired, Netherlands

My idea is to restore an old cargo ship. It would be repainted all in white, symbolic of the peace dove, and would have the task of successively going to all the large and medium-size ports of the world. Symphony concerts would be held there for the benefit of world peace. As cargo boats always have four large decks these would be reconstructed to make a concert hall, an exhibition area and bookshop with the other two decks being set aside to receive voluntary gifts of all kinds: clothes, medicines, tools, furniture, shoes, toys, food products, books, games, medical equipment, agricultural machinery etc. All these would be gathered together, sorted and renovated on board. The goal would be summarized by the slogan: "The Excesses of the Rich are the Necessities of the Poor." All the items collected in all the ports would then be given to developing third world countries.

André Gallard, Retired Sailor, France

"We are the Rubbish Collectors", Children Celebrating
Life Day, Argentina

The Global Cooperation Project may consider the setting up of
"Vision Laboratories" or "Vision Institutes" in various countries
throughout the world, where demonstrations could be shown (free) to
visitors from different walks of life (as in a museum) as to how the benefits
of Science, Technology, Medicine, Education and Cultural activities are,
and can be, helpful in actually securing the most basic human needs,
such as low-cost, but durable, aesthetically satisfying shelters; clean,
tasty, healthy food; abundant and pure drinking water; easy, inexpensive,
reliable access to facilities for maintaining and improving health, and
enhancement of the pleasure in living.

A. M. Zahoorul Huq, Professor Emeritus, Bangladesh

One hundred and five participants from government departments,
the fields of education, media and industry, and all environmental
organizations in Hong Kong contributed their ideas and experiences at
an Environmental Symposium held in response to a deep concern for the
state of Hong Kong's environment. Their appeal to all citizens included
the following:

* Encourage environmental awards e.g. Housekeeper's Award,
  Governor's Green Award, Architect's/Engineer's "ECO" Design
  Award, "Captain Planet Award."
* Encourage a pollution index to be announced in all media
  weather reports.
* Encourage the setting up of environmental information kiosks in
  shopping malls.
* Encourage the use of comic strips for environmental education.
* Encourage a metropolitan street tree project.
* Propose a ban on junk mail.
* Encourage traffic free zones.
* Encourage rezoning/relocation of industry.
* Encourage environmental awareness in families through "A Good
  Deed A Day" project.
* Remember when you "throw things away" that there is no such
  thing as "away" - it has to go somewhere!

(from the workshop report by Beverley Murphy, Hong Kong)

Creation and establishment of international taxation to achieve the goal of the Global Vision: the tax shall be defined on the basis of GNP size per capita and shall be charged on every country and district.

Y. Mizukoshi, Architect and Planner, Japan

Citizens Against Narcotics and The National Union of Public Workers, the leaders of both of which were members of the Barbados Global Cooperation Coordinating Committee, together with other committee members, devised a drug prevention project. The project's aim was to give each child within the school system (over 85,000 students) a Declaration containing a commitment from the adults of Barbados to provide an environment free from the menace of drugs. Most schools participated in the project and scrolls featuring the Declaration, set out below, were presented to each child, often in the presence of parents and members of the School's Board of Management. The students expressed delight at receiving the scrolls and many of them pledged to stay away from drugs. Their comments included:

1. We want to be taught how to say "NO" to drugs.
2. I want to live a happy, healthy life.
3. Drugs is the main thing which will prevent me from achieving my goal in life.
4. Every time I see the scroll I will be reminded not to take drugs.

On the adult level, a change has been observed by those within the schools and whereas drug abuse was seen as a sin, it is now being looked at more as an ailment or a disease. This change in vision naturally affected attitudes towards victims of drugs or would-be users.

Myrna Belgrave, Principal, Barbados

DECLARATION

To the Children of Barbados

We the Concerned Citizens Pledge that:

We shall do all that is within our power in the anti-drug campaign;

We shall cooperate to protect you from the terrible effects of drug abuse, from the suffering caused by deadly diseases and from the confusion brought about by negative attitudes;

We shall provide a way for you to use your inner talents so that you can better understand how special and beautiful you are deep within;

We shall show you positive visions and attitudes so that you can experience the inner peace and happiness that can help you to rise above the difficulties which you face and which seem to have no end;

We too have a deep desire in our hearts to see you happy, healthy, and filled with enthusiasm and hope of a better vision of tomorrow's world;

May God's light always shine on your path.

Tree planting at Port Rafti, Greece, following a huge fire. (Maria Karamartzani, Greece)

1. Create a Man University, located at the U.N. Headquarters, in which man's dignity and divinity will be the core of the curriculum. The teaching corps would be gathered from amongst the soundest minds of each member nation.
2. Reform the Nobel Peace Prize. It will be decided by a joint jury, the Swedish Royal Academy and the U.N. Security Council. The award would go to the nation instead of an individual. The award would be a 20 billion dollars loan, without interest, to develop the recipient country.
3. Build a trans-Himalayan auto-route linking Asia and Europe. Call it the Love Route or Soul Route, so that people could walk from Europe to Asia and visa-versa, and without passport.
4. Build a floating tunnel linking Asia and America; perhaps San Francisco and Shanghai, so that man could walk from Europe and Asia to America.
5. Build another one linking New York and Amsterdam.

Au Duc Chinh, Teacher, Vietnam

I would like to see an international court and law-enforcement body, under the jurisdiction of the United Nations and composed of an international body of "Wise Men", which would be empowered to take a firm stand against governments which abused their own citizens or deprived them of their human rights. The powers of this court would extend also to the protection of our commonly shared planetary environment.

Jean R. Nelson, Artist, USA

A huge fire had destroyed a lot of trees and greenery in our town, Porto Rafti. Through the Association of the Residents of Porto Rafti, 20 people decided to join forces and plant 200 trees to restore the area as it was before. The Mayor supplied us with the trees and even sent some workers to help dig the earth. Unfortunately not all the trees we planted survived and so we had to replace them. I intend to keep on watering our trees as I believe they are of major importance to our existence.

Maria Karamartzani, Doctor, Greece

Before 1983 the Berlin Wall was a very sad, depressing grey monument which divided East and West, families and countries, and people naturally stayed away from it. Then in the early 80s, a seemingly "more perfected" prefabricated WALL was installed. Its even white surface was an ideal canvas on which mainly children and foreign artists, people less emotionally affected by its existence, began to draw. To actually paint your art piece on the Wall, you had to dare to get close to it because it stood on the other side of the official border.

After two years of photographing and documenting WALL ART,

I myself went to paint in the dead of night. I painted a female figure holding healing herbs among the planets of Jupiter and Saturn to remind people of the entire cosmology of all things, the beauty of living on our earth on the one hand and the idiocy of war and divisive philosophies on the other.

I hoped that my work "Positive Vibration", as I named it, would open a new window through which people could see anew the absurdity of a wall like this in our times of space science and mass communication and that positive vibration is needed to overcome this "dead end philosophy of the older generation", as I call it.

There was a saying that "painting the WALL down" was a way to overcome it. It became a collective and cooperative work. Many people got involved and the WALL attracted more and more attention. Change was accelerated as a result: because the WALL was being used as a canvas, it became less of a psychological block and people eventually lost their fear of it. Berliners and visitors began taking their children, walking their dogs and riding their bikes along the WALL.

It forced the "status quo" out of its passive indifference and prepared the ground for the UTOPIA COME TRUE: the FALL OF THE WALL, 9th November 1989.

I think we owe all the painters who participated a great deal of thanks for their contribution in bringing it down.

Breaking down the physical WALL is one thing, but I believe that it is much more important to think about the WALL in our heads, in our minds. We have far too few utopias and visions. They are what enable us to change in our multicultural world.

Let us unite, but celebrate our differences which are the colourful wealth of humankind.

Heinz J. Kuzdas, Photographer, Germany

"Positive Vibration", a mural on the Berlin Wall, Heinz Kuzdas, Germany

The Death and ill health from asthma rose sharply in Australia in the 1980s and it became the most common chronic health problem in children and adults. By the late 1980s, concern was being freely discussed by health professionals and the community in the public media. There was no national plan of action to combat the problem and the key health bodies were addressing the issue separately.

In 1988, "Global Cooperation for a Better World" approached these major organizations, offering to bring them together to run a short national multi-media awareness campaign about asthma. The "Could it be Asthma?" campaign was launched some 2 months later, co-ordinated by "Global Cooperation for a Better World" with the cooperation of health professional bodies, business and advertising organizations. Measurable improvements in awareness about asthma were achieved. More importantly, dialogue was established between bodies which had not previously communicated.

Having successfully acted as a catalyst to bring together these key national groups, and given their understanding of the potential benefit of cooperation and sharing of skills, "Global Cooperation for a Better World" then withdrew. The Thoracic Society of Australia and New Zealand, The Royal Australasian College of General Practitioners, The Pharmaceutical Society of Australia representing the health professions, and the Asthma Foundations representing the community, then formed the National Asthma Campaign. Representatives of "Global Cooperation for a Better World" with skills in strategic planning and business continued to participate. From its formative stages, the National Asthma Campaign has worked through consensus to develop further national communications programmes and has developed an Australia-wide network of volunteers working in the asthma field ready to assist in many ways.

The National Asthma Campaign is now the peak body for asthma in Australia and has acted as a catalyst to bring together other organizations at a national, state, and regional level which in turn have acted as catalysts in their areas to bring together other organizations. Information and awareness campaigns are directed at health professionals and at asthmatics.

The National Asthma Campaign encouraged the completion of a new "Australian Asthma Management Plan" which has subsequently been used as a basis of asthma care for all Australians and was the first such plan published for asthma in the world. Its wide acceptance and use as the benchmark of best practice over such a short period of time has been remarkable. Many thousands of medical practitioners, and a larger group of other health professionals, have expressed support for the Plan and the work being done by the National Asthma Campaign. There has now been a resurgence of interest and support for asthma and asthma sufferers throughout the community.

Results have been achieved by this harnessing of energies, skills and expertise. Over the last 3 years the death rate has declined by 20%, the numbers of those seeking hospital care have been reduced and there is a greater awareness of the social, personal and economic issues. The National Asthma Campaign has recieved widespread support for its work from health professionals, government and the business community.

The Australian community owes much to "Global Cooperation for a Better World" for showing what can be achieved when human beings work together through a shared vision and cooperate with each other for the the benefit of the community.

The quality of relationships which has developed has been enduring and has overcome many seemingly insurmountable obstacles. We are now in the planning stages of a National Asthma Strategy bringing together the many other community, business and health organizations to plan coopearatively for the future to create a vision for asthma.

Ral Antic, Medical Practitioner, Australia

Global Cooperation T-Shirt - a world of laughter, a world of joy. (Kris, UK)

Scientists View the Future

Fifty-two eminent scientists from twenty-two countries, and all the continents of the world, gathered in Athens, Greece in January 1990 to find and articulate ways to implement a new perspective of science and technology in the service of the world. The occasion was the International Symposium on "Science, Technology and the Environment: A Case for Global Cooperation", organized as part of the Global Cooperation project.

Four roundtable discussion groups were formed. Although each group developed its views independently, the commonality was significant and a "core" perspective emerged. All the groups placed great emphasis on high ethical values for science, its integration with social purpose, and on social responsibility and environmental sensitivity in its application. There was a call for greater integration of scientific disciplines to reduce the fragmentation of knowledge. There was also a call for a closer nexus between science and the humanities so that the way science is developed and used is more sensitive to its social context. Educational programmes which reflect these ideas were considered essential.

There was the recognition that all peoples of the world form an interdependent global community for whose benefit scientific knowledge and technology must be openly shared.

Some expressed the view that the prevailing scientific paradigm is adequate to the task of realizing the new vision. Others strongly disagreed. The following extracts from the interactions which took place give an indication of the unique flavour and diversity of ideas which were discussed by each group.

1. New Perspectives

It is necessary that the creation of new perspectives starts by addressing the problems of human behaviour. Goodwill, integrity, justice and service to others are some of the prime values which need to be cultivated to attain the desired goal of living in harmony with ourselves, other species and the natural world. Envision three concentric circles: the inner one representing the well-being of all living species; the next circle representing the interaction of the species within the respective communities; and the outermost circle representing a harmonious and ecological living within the total environment. The innermost circle deals with the individual, the next with society, and the outermost with the physical and metaphysical world.

2. To Serve Humanity

Scientific knowledge, from the moment it is created, belongs to all of humanity. It is the fruit of human history and the human brain. So justice and openness in distributing the fruits of scientific knowledge in an understandable way is an obligation of scientists so that the public is made aware of any dangers or benefits that the scientists think might result from their work. Since knowledge provides the means of using the earth's resources and also provides the means of avoiding the abuse of the environment, our commonly shared heritage, the dissemination of knowledge is a highly valued human activity.

Technology is produced by invention, mostly by the application of science. It is technology which changes the human and natural environment. There is no assurance whatever that a given technology will be a social good. It may be good, bad, or indifferent. Science should be primarily controlled internally by the scientists themselves, who should show the highest possible responsibility in choosing the directions of research, in deciding the priorities, in being honest in the way the results are produced, in the way they are interpreted and in the way they are made available to society. Openness and dialogue should prevail in examining different ideas and what we understand to be truth.

Technology must be controlled by laws and regulations - a careful analysis of the public and environmental costs and benefits in each case. It should be made clear who bears the costs and who enjoys the benefits.

3. New Realities

Our Global Vision is that there is fulfillment of the needs of the spirit, mind, body, society and the biosphere. Specifically, our vision is of a world where:

* There is a universal outlook reflecting understanding of the interrelatedness of all aspects of life.
* Ideas, knowledge, human and natural resources are exchanged among different cultures without barriers and this flow is governed by values such as tolerance, humility and mutual respect for diversity.

* The social and humanistic sciences take responsibility in developing value systems based on individual and social needs and offering their expertise to the natural sciences and technology in the service of the world.

4. Ethics of Science

That science:
* have respect for life;
* be applied in its cultural framework;
* incorporate social participation in its development;
* be cognisant of its long-term implications.

from the Conference Report prepared and edited by Stella E. Humphries, Environmental Scientist, Australia; the conference, inspired by Global Cooperation, has now become an annual event.

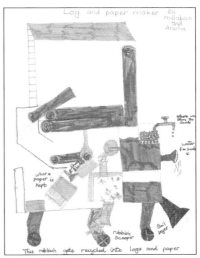

Log and Paper Machine, Mayabeen and Arusha, Coston School, Ages 9 and 10, UK

Conference Reflections

What impressed me most was how there were more than fifty of us from all over the world, with widely different backgrounds, spanning the whole spectrum of political persuasion, and yet there was overwhelming agreement as to what we all want. I don't mean just clean air, clean water, clean food, adequate housing and an unpolluted environment. I mean the general realization that in order to guarantee all of those things for ourselves, we have to guarantee them for everybody else on earth. And that is the fundamental basis for global cooperation: the acknowledgment that we are all interconnected with nature as interdependent parts of one global ecosystem. Whatever is done in one part of the world will have repercussions not only locally, but globally as well. The excessive consumption of fossil fuels in the industrialized West and the destruction of tropical forests in South America are both cases in point in their contribution to global warming. This message is particularly relevant for those of us who are inhabitants of the affluent first and second worlds much of whose affluence has been built upon the exploitation of the third world in colonial and postcolonial times.

There was also broad agreement that much of the prevailing science and technology is exploitative and destructive and needs to be phased out in favour of new sciences and technologies that are caring and protective of life and the environment. I use the plurals deliberately in order to draw attention to many traditional indigenous sciences and technologies which have a lot to teach us in the way of how to live in harmony with nature and with one another, but which have been displaced and in many instances destroyed by western science and technology.

Mae-Wan Ho, Biophysicist, UK

Section 2 - The Principles of Cooperation

*W*orking together is not always easy and at different stages in the Global Cooperation project groups got together to draw up basic principles of cooperation - approaches and ways of doing things that are an indispensable part of working together and that can help translate visions from concepts into reality.

Like the visions, the principles were the same the world over regardless of continent, race, religion or politics; principles which work in village conflicts are equally valid in drawn out international negotiations. In whatever way they are interpreted in the hundreds of tongues across the continents of the world, the same essential ingredients emerged. These common components were synthesized into "The Principles of Cooperation" which are set out below together with some examples of practical experiences of cooperation.

THE PRINCIPLES OF COOPERATION

I.   In any endeavour the hopes, needs and common goals of those concerned are clearly identified and communicated.

II.   Cooperation between individuals and groups is a voluntary process based on tolerance, understanding, mutual benefit and respect.

III. In every endeavour there is a sense of honesty and trust between partners in cooperation.

IV.   Recognizing the fundamental dignity of each human being, all rise above narrow considerations and work together in a spirit of harmony.

V.   The process of cooperation is enhanced by the reduction of any tension through mental relaxation, positive thinking and quiet reflection.

VI.   The contribution of each person or group of people is considered integral to the accomplishment of any cooperative task.

VII. There is individual and collective responsibility in any cooperative decisions and actions.

VIII. All listen to and acknowledge the views and ideas of others in any cooperative task.

Global cooperation is not a fun fair nor even the celebrations of those self and mutually laudatory "good" souls. It is rather a joining of anxious hearts the world over determined to get to grips with problems suicidal to our own and to every life on earth, problems which simply cannot be resolved by any means short of total global cooperation of men, women and children: ergo cooperation between real and potential enemies; a total cooperation by conviction - but also by constraint and enforcement.

Global cooperation is a call for conviction, out-spokenness, deep, compassionate and practical thought and ACTION.

Lord Menuhin, UK

I

In any endeavour the hopes, needs and common goals of those concerned are clearly identified and communicated.

For years our two neighbouring communities in San Ignacio Mixco were at loggerheads over the local sanitary conditions. There were no paved streets, no public lighting system and no drainage system. Finally we stepped in and cooperation saved the day. We organized regular meetings to understand each other's viewpoints and needs, and met with the municipal authorities to sort out finances. Within twelve months the community had light, water, wide streets and drainage.

Aminta Leon and Anne Bonin, Guatemala

I set out for Machakos in the company of Elizabeth Kotut, Joan Ahero and Ndunda Kiema. Ndunda is an acquaintance from Nairobi whose native home is in Iiani, a small village about one and a half kilometers from Machakos town. The climate is hot throughout the year and there is a scarcity of rain. The soil however is very fertile and this is an agricultural area very productive in maize, sogam, wheat, coffee and citrus fruits. The natives, the Akamba tribe, are considered to be a very progressive tribe of good political, social and economic status. They are very well informed people and education is readily available up to primary school, and higher levels. The houses are mostly made of corrugated iron or thatched grass as a protection from the heat. The main water supply is from the Athi River. The people bore holes and irrigate the land. A good supply of water also comes from the tanks on the rooftops of houses, where rainwater collects. Water from the Government Municipality is not readily available.

On arrival at Iiani, we were welcomed by Ndunda's family. Ndunda quickly sent a message across to his friends calling a meeting for 3.00 p.m. In no time the entire neighbourhood had been alerted and a group of twenty-five people soon assembled.

A newly finished water tank being put to use, Machakos, Kenya. (Shobna Obhrai, Kenya)

VISIONS OF A BETTER WORLD

Farming in Machakos, Kenya. (Shobna Obhrai, Kenya)

For them, development was carried out on a physical level only through material assistance. In their dictionary, a better world meant better times in life with easy access to the basic needs. Asked what they thought to be the most significant problem that they were facing they hastily answered "water!" They complained of having a poor harvest every time the rains failed. After relating examples of the sort of cooperation Global Cooperation sought, the group was very enthusiastic and ready to jump into action. Ndunda suggested that a cooperative plan be undertaken to help relieve the water shortage. The approach would be to build storage tanks in which rainwater would collect. For this, stones, sand and cement were required. The group decided to collect money from amongst themselves to buy cement and together collect the stones and sand from the river bank. They would then build the tanks together.

Over the months Ndunda has been keeping in close contact with the group during his visits home. Suggestions have been pouring in. One member felt that if more money could be raised, they could buy pumps to bore the water from sub-surface rivers. The group also promised to remain cooperative in all aspects of life and encourage others to join in with them. They would now do things collectively - growing vegetables, collecting water and so on. About five tanks were built in the first ten months and many were on the way. When an aged member of the group fell ill Ndunda was fascinated to learn that the group pulled in money to enable him to be hospitalized.

They all concluded that this was the beginning of a new relationship between themselves. They were already friends no doubt, but never have they felt so close to each other and concerned about each other's needs.

Shobna Obhrai, Legal Assistant, Kenya

II

**Cooperation between individuals and groups is a voluntary process
based on tolerance, understanding, mutual benefit and respect.**

To me, roots for the future stand on equity, caring and sharing.
This vision of a better world is shared by many individuals making up
the constituency of Non-Governmental organizations and community
groups. To us, individuals in their homes, in their communities and
places of work have rights which they expect in their relations with
each other at family level - where should I have my cigarette; should I
even smoke? with their neighbours and communities - what would
happen to the ecosystem if I destroy the vegetation cover? what if I
empty my pesticide residues in the river? do I violate other people's
rights by meeting my perceived needs in certain ways?

But to me, this caring can only be meaningful if people are able
to meet their most urgent and perceived needs. I am talking about
issues of equity and of sharing. Today, I see a world divided between
the haves and have nots; more than this between the over-consumers
and the under-consumers. A better world, I see, is one where the
over-consumers de-develop so that portions of what they would consume
is shared out to the under-consumers. For resources are all finite and
we must guard them. One's responsibilities then stretch out to others
and to nature to enable us to reach a better world. We all must learn
ethics built on "me-and-the-other" and not "me alone". Only such
foundations can help us build a world of sharing which is an important basis for sustainability of resources and societies.

I am talking about equity. For a sustainable world and society
must ensure that assets, power, information, skills all have to be
distributed if not equally but equitably. Unless every person has
access to assets to ensure their livelihoods, then we cannot claim
hopes of a better future.

Farming in Machakos, Kenya. (Shobna Obhrai, Kenya)

In the majority of cases, most power holders have over-stretched their sense of responsibility to include the right to know what others need. Thus policy-makers have excluded the majority of citizens in decision-making regarding policies friendly to end-users. Scientists and technologists have developed technology on the assumptions that the majority end-users are ignorant. Now, we know this not to be the case. Many Non-Governmental organizations are steps ahead of other brokers in recognizing this. Many are listening to the people. A few see the value of building on people's experiences and experiments, interacting with those for a sustainable future. The Environment Liaison Centre International, with which I worked for five years and of whose experiences I can speak with authority, has for two years facilitated national, regional and interregional consultations on people's participation in environmentally sustainable development. These consultations brought together 20-30 people from different sectors of society - rural and urban community women and men, NGO representatives, peasant farmers, fisher persons, large-scale farmers, governmental policy-makers, law-makers, university researchers and technologists. They came to share their vision of a better world and how to get there.

At the end of one such consultation, one technologist declared that he had been empowered. After three days of listening to and sharing ideas with rural and urban women and men, he felt he would go back to his laboratories with a different approach, an approach of interacting with the knowledge of the local people who had been managing the environment for centuries. A village woman left another consultation a happier person because she had managed to convince NGOs of the need to listen to the people in whose name they carry out projects. She was also happier because the whole group asked itself whether indeed terms such as participate are themselves not questionable as they assume that others set agendas for beneficiaries in which agendas/ projects the latter participate.

The final test of commitment to a better world by all will come when rich countries accept that the world has reached a stage where they cannot expand anymore; where rich people everywhere learn to cut down their levels of resource consumption to enable access to assets by all; where we all learn to listen to each other, especially to the poor and marginalized. This is happening among some NGOs. We need to spread the ethics of caring and sharing to all NGOs, communities and governments. But all institutions are made up of people, therefore the starting point should be at the individual level. Individual responsibility especially of the rich, the policy-makers and decision-makers is the firm basis of a better world.

Shimwaayi Muntemba, Director-General, Earthcare Africa, Zambia

III

In every endeavour there is a sense of honesty and trust between partners in cooperation.

The Shoeshine Boys, Brazil. (Simone Boger, Brazil)

Tucked away at the back of a dilapidated building in the sugarcane belt city of Piracicaba, Sao Paulo state, an old shed acts as the temporary meeting and meal place of 80 children and adolescents aged between 8 and 16. For years this "Shoeshine Boys' Club", established by the local Lion's Club, has been spartanly sustained by the town council and voluntary contributions. Besides removing from the hazards of the streets these children, whose families struggle to survive below the poverty line, the "club" provides the working materials that are needed for their daily routine. In a country where there are literally millions of abandoned and poor children living on the streets, it's a brave attempt at returning a few of them to a little dignity.

"Not one of our children sniffs glue or smokes marijuana", says social-worker Maria Angela Calore, proud of these kids saved from having to beg or steal for a living. These children, adults long before their time, showed a core of solidarity amongst themselves that reflected their "stand" in a world that offers rare favours.

The spontaneity and enthusiasm with which they described their vision were in sharp contrast to their daily grind, literally at the feet of society. "Earth is a beautiful place." "Cooperation is when we are all as friends." "Lending your work materials is cooperation, to give polish, lend a brush, to be a friend." "We wish humanity well and especially the earth." "Clean the world." Many illustrated their visions of a greener and more vibrant nature. They all wanted to play a part in a world which had "asphalt streets full of colourful brick houses and flower-laden walls".

Education, friendship, discipline, non-violence and especially better individual behaviour were the values they considered as most important to bring about a better world. Thus these shoeshine boys, who barely earn enough to keep the shirts on their backs, and who in many cases are the only source of income for the rest of their family, have shown that the better world will definitely have a bigger heart - certainly as big as their hopes.

Ken O'Donnell, Writer, Brazil

IV

**Recognizing the fundamental dignity of each human being, all
rise above narrow considerations and work
together in a spirit of harmony.**

Malaysia is made up of three main ethnic groups: the Malays, the
Chinese and the Indians. Islam is the State religion, with religious
freedom existing alongside.

We had a programme arranged at the Malaysian Institute of Art
to introduce Global Cooperation. The students came up with an idea
of painting the biggest painting for peace in Malaysia. They designed
a painting called "Global Vision" to measure 120ft. by 90ft. and to be
sectioned into 1,200 three-foot squares of plywood so that the 1,200
students of the Institute could paint it in one day. The event was
timed to coincide with a meeting of the Commonwealth Heads of
Government in Kuala Lumpur on the 19th October 1989. The whole
Institute, right up to the Dean, was involved. ICI Ltd. supplied 420
litres of paint in various colours; the Malaysian Plywood
Manufacturers Association donated the wood.

Malaysians are a family, a family of different races. The majority
of the students participating were of one race. Members of the working
committee felt that the beauty of this natural blend of the various
races and the combined family spirit would be obscured, and so with
united feelings an invitation was extended to Malay students of
MARA Institute of Technology for their participation.

The students had learned that cooperation means getting everyone
together. It is a sign of love. They understood that it wasn't some
kind of ego trip and that their cooperation, their working together

> The Global Vision is
> not merely a painting but
> the pride and dignity of
> Malaysian youth. It is a
> living memorial of the
> unity of our people and the
> hope of peace and love for
> every citizen in the world.
> *Dr. Siti Hasmah Bte Haji
> Mohd Ali, wife of the
> Prime Minister of Malaysia*

Students working on the "Global Vision" peace painting, in Merdeka Square, Kuala
Lumpur, Malaysia.

The creation of the 120 ft. by 90 ft. "Global Vision" peace painting by 1,200 young artists in Merdeka Square, Kuala Lumpur, Malaysia.

was more significant - and that's why through all the trials, they stuck together. They immediately agreed for 600 students from the Institute to step down so that students from the MARA Institute of Technology could replace them. It was an amazing act of sacrifice, seeing that they had invested so much of themselves for nearly a year in the project.

But problems developed behind the scenes when the MARA Institute students saw a model of the painting after the press conference. They said the design along the border of the painting was slightly contrary to Islamic beliefs and wanted to change the border design into something more abstract. The students from the Malaysian Institute of Art agreed to give over the painting for redesign. It was just two or three days before the event. All the pieces of the painting had already been numbered and arranged in sequence, so the changes to the border meant changes to the entire layout. This meant working day and night to alter the design in time; this was completed, but only the day before the event.

The event took place in Merdeka Square in the centre of Kuala Lumpur. From conception to completion, it had taken almost a whole year to prepare for that final day, but the actual painting was done in just one hour. Each student picked up one square and painted it with the specified colours. Then they came one by one and laid the pieces down line by line. It was quite a sight to see 1,200 people, dressed in the same T-shirts, which ICI had provided to promote a cooperative team spirit, working under the steaming sun. The completed painting was spread out on the lush, green lawn for everyone to see and made front page coverage in all the national press.

A smaller version of the 120 ft. by 90 ft. "Global Vision" peace painting by 1,200 young artists in Merdeka Square, Kuala Lumpur, Malaysia.

Yeoh Jin Leng, Dean of Studies of the Malaysian Institute of Art said: "The project should be seen as a catalyst to develop further our commitment towards cooperation. Problems in this world are human ones and they are to say the least confusingly complex. Wisdom, and sometimes courage, are essential ingredients that have to be applied in the process. The cooperation given by everyone is to be commended. I am enriched in experience and have come closer to understanding human relationships at different levels."

The willing hand of support extended by the MARA students and the unwavering will of the MIA students that the project should succeed brought about a delightful friendship between the students of the two colleges and a keen awareness of the power that cooperation brings.

On 13th August 1991 Datin Seri Dr. Siti Hasmah, wife of the Prime Minister of Malaysia, presented a replica of the painting, with the flags of all the Commonwealth countries bordering it, to Foreign Minister Datuk Abdullah Ahmad Badawi. Accepting the painting before a gathering of politicians, diplomats and others, Datuk Abdullah Ahmad Badawi said "the replica was a testimony of perpetual commitment to global peace and would be displayed in the Treaty Room at the Foreign Ministry as a constant reminder of the shared vision of young Malaysians."

Parameshvari Kanniah, with Felicia Chong and Shamsiah Sanin, Journalists, Malaysia

Miniature painting of "Global Vision" in the Treaty Room Wisma Putra, Ministry of Foreign Affairs, following its presentation to the Minister of Foreign Affairs by Global Cooperation patron-in-chief Dr. Siti Hasmah, wife of the Prime Minister of Malaysia.
L. to R.: Datin Seri Dr. Siti Hasmah, Mrs. P.G. Lim (Chair, Global Cooperation Advisory Committee, Malaysia), Datuk Abdullah bin Haji Ahmad Badawi (Minister of Foreign Affairs) and Tengku Dato Ahmad Rithauddeen (President of U.N. Malaysia Association)

V

The process of cooperation is enhanced by the reduction of any tension through mental relaxation, positive thinking and quiet reflection.

Various negative experiences were forcing me to find a solution for myself. I thought I must start with myself in my home before I can share anything with others outside. Global Cooperation gave me the final push to create a peaceful room in our house in which only positive conversation, prayer or meditation would be allowed. I was surprised to see that all of the family respected this room from the moment I told them about it. By keeping complaints and criticisms out of this room it has become like an oasis of peace that helps us to come together as a family and solve daily problems in a peaceful way. My daughter Alexandra told me "from this experience of peace and communication that has developed through the positive room, I have become better in my school and in my dealings with friends". For my part I have gained greater self control and have stopped smoking.

Despina Iacumaki, Housewife, Greece

Applying the "be positive" golden rule of Global Cooperation can sometimes prove to be a challenge. We were unexpectedly invited to visit the Mashabo Mission, an Amerindian community in Essequibo, a county of Guyana, by local authority officers. To get there is an 8 mile walk along a lonely jungle track full of potholes and ditches. Amerindians are considered aboriginals, natives, often overlooked by the world. They live as a closely knit family very suspicious of strangers and rarely leave their communities. They would hardly ever dream of visiting towns or cities.

As we made our way through the dense jungle the only sound was the echo of our own voices as we sang and shared light experiences to help make the journey easier. At the end of the track we rowed across a beautiful and inviting lake to reach the community. Doors and windows of thatched-roof bungalows slammed shut as we approached. However, after a discussion between the Captain of the community and the local officers he and his group became extremely warm and welcoming and we relaxed. Many of the people were at first too shy even to look at us and never attempted to come close. Perhaps because of our seemingly peaceful attitude and harmless intentions their shyness was gradually replaced by curiosity and an atmosphere of faith and trust was soon created. Coordinating the workshop, I found myself having to be extremely gentle. I think that

**Creative Group with
Amerindians, Guyana**

the few moments of silence, with which we began the discussion, touched them deeply. Because of their simple life-style and closeness to nature silence seems to mean a lot to them. It took a while for communication to flow but eventually it seemed natural for them.

The Captain offered his vision of a better world to start the discussion and spoke of a better self being an example by which others' faith in him would grow. He felt that self respect was the key factor to enable him to achieve his goal. As others began to share their vision the commitment and sincerity of their words made a strong impact on me which stays with me to this day.

Deokie Ramsahai, Social Worker, Guyana

Creative Group with Amerindians, Guyana.

VI

The contribution of each person or group of people is considered integral to the accomplishment of any cooperative task.

I live on the island of Mindanao in the south of the Philippines in a slum area of Surigao City known as Sabang. Ten thousand people live in very small shanty homes built of plywood or cardboard with dried palm leaves for roofs. It's a desolate place to live, and a violent province. Our monastery can only be reached by walking over a footbridge from the main road and then traversing narrow planks across muddy waters. The whole place is surrounded by refuse and swamps and every year a typhoon comes and they have to rebuild their houses.

The people I work with are overwhelmed by their poverty. They have no sense of vision or direction in their lives. Their awareness is only up to the next meal, which they usually get from combing the refuse. It's really hard for them to think about the future because they exist from one meal to another.

Even though it was all new to me, creating a vision sparked off a whole chain of events in my community. I got the young sisters involved straight away. We spent seven days discussing our vision of how we would like to see ourselves, our community and the world. Some of the girls were as young as 16 and I had lived with them for eight years but never imagined they could have a vision of a world without slums. They said "everyday this vision will grow and become a reality." Things started to change immediately. They realized how important it was to spread the message of cleanliness to the slum dwellers. If a sister got sick they would try to help her and not just wait for medicine.

Although they are very needy the poor can be the best examples of sharing and service to others. I've got couples coming together to create their vision of a better family, and mothers to create theirs of a better neighbourhood. A group of neighbours were inspired to get proper training and are learning soap-making and candle-making so that eventually they can earn a living. Their example is having a positive impact on others in the community. People are seeing that it is possible for them to improve their lot and lead a different life.

It's so important to see the poor as being able to make an important contribution to the world and not just to position them on the receiving end of what the world is prepared to give. The poor can play a leadership role in peace building just like anyone else. Fatalism is very strong in the slums. It's such a crippling attitude because it prevents people from believing they can do anything about their situation.

Creative Group with parapalegics at our Lady of Victory Training Centre, Mindanao, Philippines. The participants were inspired to remain positive instead of focusing on their problems. (Rebecca R. Ortega, Philippines)

At present we are preparing to move into a farm which we ourselves will till. Planting the fruits and vegetables we eat, planting mini forests, and living in harmony with the animals and other creatures allows us to live a life that is not only healthy for the body and the mind but even more so a deeply spiritual life lived in simplicity and in close union with God and the whole of creation. This is our first step of our contribution in the building up of a better world for our one global family.

Sister Rose Mary, Directress, The Little Servants of the Blessed Trinity, Philippines

VII

There is individual and collective responsibility in any cooperative decisions and actions.

Jordan has one million young people out of a total population of four million and by the end of 1989 the Teachers Pack "Cooperation in the Classroom" had reached nearly all of Amman's one thousand schools. Each workshop with one of the trained scouts or guides resulted in eight more as each participant then led their own workshop with their friends or family. We also collected 18,000 visions of a better world from children across Jordan and exhibited some of the best in an Amman art gallery. All of this resulted in many practical actions.

As one action plan young guides and scouts collected toys, clothes and sweets which Princess Basma personally gave to six hundred orphaned or handicapped children. Other scouts and guides wanted to make a park for the handicapped and with the help of one of the Amman Town Hall engineers, Mr. Baakir Alibadhe, a big park was created. It's the first park for the handicapped in Jordan, has fruit trees and swings and two days a week a different scout troop goes to look after it. In some schools students started looking after the school garden or even laid one out. In one school each pupil donated a book to start a library, while in another school a group was inspired to clean the shores of the Dead Sea. The action plans were very varied. One girl in a village in South Jordan visited a poor family to share her vision of the need for better education for women and persuaded the parents to allow their daughters to seek higher education. From

Students participating in tree planting for the Greener Jordan Campaign, Jordan.
(Abla Abu-Nowar, Jordan)

Young girls participating in the Keep Jordan Clean Campaign, Jordan.
(Abla Abu-Nowar, Jordan)

Young boys participating in tree planting for the Greener Jordan Campaign, Jordan.
(Abla Abu-Nowar, Jordan)

another workshop came the vision of a cleaner Jordan and a "Keep Jordan Clean" campaign was soon started. It was a great success and three million plastic bags were collected. Inspired by this success, the Ministry of Education, in cooperation with the Ministry of Agriculture, decided to involve the whole country in planting trees for a greener Jordan. Fourteen year old Mazen Ahmed Flyhei reported on this as follows:

"'Green is happiness and beauty is as warm as life. Green is alive and loving like hope, the future.' With such words the Green Jordan 2000 campaign was initiated through the Boy Scouts and Girl Guides of Jordan. The aim of the project is to make all the land green and fertile with a beautiful forest that will attract rain. The greenery protects the land from becoming barren thus enabling the land to be fertile. All the government participated in planting trees, right up to H.M. King Hussein. I am one of the honoured citizens who participated in this campaign and this working together brought about so much happiness amongst us as we gave life back to the land. We treated the land gently as though we were putting the treasure of life back in her."

During the campaign one million young people each planted a tree and encouraged their families to do the same. Each student looks after the tree he or she planted. We are going to carry on planting trees until it is green in Jordan.

Abla Abu-Nowar, Head of Girl Guides and Boy Scouts, Jordan

VIII

All listen to and acknowledge the views and ideas of others in any cooperative task.

Siena College of Taytay was established in 1957 by the Dominican Sisters to provide elementary, secondary and tertiary education to residents of 7 towns along the Laguna Lake area 35 kilometers from Metropolitan Manila. Siena's total school enrollment is about 2,100 with about 100 teaching and other staff.

Trouble started in 1987 when a new principal made unpopular personnel decisions which were seen by staff as labour harassment and gave rise to great tension and animosity to the detriment of students and parents alike. Then a newly formed union of some of the teachers started a picket line which led to a two-week strike and ended with a court case reinstating some dismissed strikers. The whole experience was so negative that the school administration decided to allow present students to graduate but then to close the school.

However, at the request of the new President of the College a six hour Global Cooperation workshop for a better workplace was held as part of staff in-service training in June 1989. The 100 teaching and other staff were divided into groups of ten and asked to:
- create and discuss their vision of a better workplace;
- identify specific values and aspects of the vision; and
- prepare a 5 minute group presentation of their vision in any form such as song, sketch, drawing or dance.

Creative Group with staff on strike from Siena School, Philippines. (Rebecca R. Ortega, Philippines)

The group-work and presentation proved to be the turning point of the day. The indifferent and almost hostile atmosphere began to change as the staff shared their hopes and dreams of a better workplace. During the presentation laughter and giggles filled the air in acknowledgment of the talents shown by the different groups. By lunchtime there were more smiling faces and a much lighter interaction. After lunch participants planned how to translate their vision of peace, love, harmony, cooperation, professionalism, God-loving community, and clean and green environment into action. Each group formulated a plan of action specific to their needs and concerns.

By the day's end the majority of the staff said that the workshop made it possible to work again in a happy and cooperative atmosphere after two and a half years of conflict and animosity. In the process of creating their vision they had begun to experience what it means to cooperate, communicate and interact in harmony. They were now ready to forget all that had happened in the past and looked forward to a better Siena. Three follow-up workshops were held in August and November 1989 and March 1990. The November workshop was a cause for celebration as all agreed that the past five months had been full of achievements ranging from improved relationships, through better work and learning atmosphere, and working results to a happy and vibrant Siena community. In December the administration announced that the decision to close the school was reversed and that new students would be accepted.

Rebecca R. Ortega, Human Resource Consultant, Philippines

School children after a creative group in Perth, Australia. (G.B. Jarman, Australia)

CHAPTER SIX

THE
VISIONS
OF
LEADERS

Once upon a time there lived a beautiful world, a happy world. The sun shone on it all the time; everyone loved it and it belonged to everyone.

People in every country yearn for a world free from hunger, fear and danger. There is much that people of goodwill can do to advance these objectives.

The Rt. Hon. Malcolm Fraser, C.H., Australia

We did not so much receive the earth, our village, from our parents but in fact borrowed it from our children.

It is our duty to make and keep the world community of nations and people a better place to live in. Peace and security, economic growth and employment, social justice and cultural development, equality of chances and liberty of opinion are the essential values to be promoted all over the world, not only in speeches but in daily activity as well. It is much easier to love mankind than to love the people you live or work with every day.

The inhabitants of the highly industrialized countries are especially responsible, not only because they are more prosperous than the rest of the world, but also because they are responsible for the armament race in the world, as a result of their own history, and for the bringing about of the weapons for the Last Judgment.

For this reason the industrialized countries have to take their cooperation with the countries of the third world seriously and improve it in a structural manner.

Mark Eyskens, Belgium

Respect for the rights of man and respect for the uniqueness of each individual form the base for real peace. Peace of this kind will also result in a righteous world order. International togetherness and understanding among people and countries will reinforce solidarity and deepen peace more.

Leo Tindemans, Belgium

Man seems to have a propensity for self-destruction and because of this, the world has been rendered or made more and more a precarious place for the continued existence of man. Since we triggered the foregoing, it is only us who can reverse the trend.

We should therefore all work towards and be committed to the elimination of all that man has brought into existence which is inconsistent with the peaceful and harmonious existence of man.

President Q. K. J. Masire, Botswana

My vision of this world's future is rooted in my firm belief that justice, defined in its broadest sense, is central to a new world order. My vision is also based on the conviction that practical solutions for the serious problems facing us are within our grasp. We have the technology needed to feed ourselves, to manage our natural environment, to abolish weapons of mass destruction, to immunize and educate our children, and to end discrimination based on gender, race or other grounds.

The promise lies before us of an international order which allows the peoples of the world to have greater confidence in the future. That order must be based on a respect of different cultures and values, in an equitable sharing of the planet's resources, and in the right of all to participate democratically in the governance of their society. The realization of that promise will not be easy, but it is a vision worth achieving.

Brian Mulroney, Canada

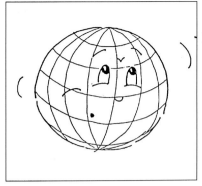

But gradually, as must happen, the world grew older.

A s we learn from the experience of history, without democracy there can be economic prosperity for a certain time but it will not lay down permanent roots because the lack of freedom will foster abuse of the weak by the powerful.

Without economic growth, on the other hand, there can be democracy, but the well-intentioned efforts to improve the living standards of the underprivileged segments of the population will lead to serious economic crises that shake the social system and, naturally, jeopardize democracy itself.

Without social justice, there is the ever-present threat in any democracy, no matter how thriving, that the natural restlessness of the underprivileged sectors clamouring for equal treatment may disturb the processes of economic development, so that the stability of the political systems hangs in the balance.

We have learned that if democracy as a form of political coexistence is reconciled with economic growth and with social justice, all individuals will be living under the conditions of freedom and justice that they require to develop their full potential and to make this a better world.

President Patricio Aylwin, Chile

E veryone has the obligation to dedicate intellectual and material resources to the discussion and development of solutions to humanity's most pressing problems. The search for peace is intimately linked to the problems of poverty, environmental deterioration, underdevelopment, racism and totalitarianism. The continuation of that marvellous adventure known as civilization will be impossible if we do not give up the use of force and begin to act in solidarity, despite borders and philosophical, ideological or religious differences.

We live on a planet that is becoming smaller; one in which countries, communities and individuals are becoming more and more interdependent. Today, every human being contributes to the fate of every other one of his fellow human beings. No leader of our era can ignore the obligation of knowing what is occurring in every part of the world, of knowing the thoughts, actions and aspirations of

Then one day something terrible happened. Dark clouds of negativity came and surrounded the world and blocked out the sunlight.

all cultures and of all nations. Today's problems no longer affect just one country or one region. We are all aware that as we confront our common problems and threats we must search for collective solutions. Never before has the human race been so convinced that it cannot delay the creation of an alliance for mutual defence comprised by all people and nations.

The concept of mutual defence reminds us of the bitter aggression and hostility that continues to be a part of our daily lives. In the past, mutual defence often served as an excuse for war. The word "defence," a word indisputably linked to the term "security," has always had a predominantly military connotation. The institutions and resources that nations dedicate to aggression are presented as institutions and resources of defence that guarantee security. We speak of national defence and security as fundamental forces behind the most important events of our time, and we build a dangerous mythology full of prejudices, sectarianism, nationalism and arrogance around these terms. Under the false pretext of guaranteeing national defence and security, the world has not only ignored the real natural threats against human life, but has created others that are more complex and dangerous.

Science allows us to have a detailed and trustworthy vision of the geological history and biological limitations of our planet. It reveals that nature itself contains serious threats endangering the human race, as well as all animal and plant species. Humanity's greatest efforts should be dedicated to guaranteeing defence and security before these enemies. Humanity should unite and develop a defence plan, a security strategy against the threats of inequality, ignorance, disease, poverty, and environmental decay. But the concepts of defence and security that the leaders of the world have been proposing, not only have made us neglect these threats against humanity, but also have produced more urgent ones: the arms race, militarization, poverty intensified by wasted resources, and the aftermath of oppression, destruction and death provoked by war. This is an appropriate occasion to reflect on the need for the people of industrialized and developing nations to come together to combat militarism and the buildup of arms, to establish the basis for a pact of security and mutual defence that includes all human beings.

Oscar Arias Sanchez, Nobel laureate, Costa Rica

We must try to close the gap between knowledge and practice. Everything must be done to ensure that environmental matters become a way of life, not something that we listen to and discuss. People must be made aware that conservation is good, and not something the government forces the people to do.

President Sir Clarence Seignoret, Commonwealth of Dominica

My vision of a better world is one in which there is an abiding respect for the life and dignity of the individual and his full development in ample social and economic conditions. To enable each individual to play a constructive role in society, it is essential that leaders promote a global environment of peace and security, free from the scourge of war, hunger and disease. In this environment, social and economic justice must be a high priority.

Hugh Desmond Hoyte, Guyana

Personally, I believe building up confidence between people of different nationalities to be of great importance. Freedom to travel and to get to know each other is, in my mind, most important in order to counter prejudice and all kinds of misunderstandings. Freedom, in general, might be listed among the priorities. It is fine and even necessary to have a vision, this I strongly support, but it is also important to map a road toward realization of that vision.

Steingrimur Hermannsson, Iceland

Throughout human history we have seen times of peace and times of war. But in my mind even the times of peace that we have seen have seldom really been times when we have been at peace with ourselves. Unless we change this basic thinking, until we break this mindset, we are not going to have what we call "shanti" in India. Superficially, the word means "peace" but it has a deeper meaning. You cannot have shanti unless the way the human mind thinks is altered.

When I go to our villages I find among the poorest, the worst-off, people who are happy and smiling. There is a certain spirituality, a certain fulfillment. You can see it on their faces, you can see it in their behaviour. And then you go to another area, where what we call development has taken place, and nobody is really happy. They are scowling, they are frowning, they are not at peace with themselves. And how can anybody who is not at peace with himself create peace in the world?

Rajiv Gandhi, India

One cannot fail to recall with profound gratification the astounding recent victory of freedom of expression, movement and action in Eastern and Central Europe. Europe and the world have made a gigantic step towards a better future for humanity. The model of European change will, we pray, be followed in the Middle East as well, and move the centre of gravity in political life there from violence, aggression and hostile threats, to a genuine desire for negotiation and understanding. Inner, as well as international

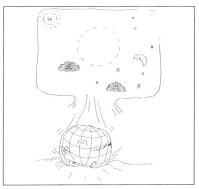

The darkness of negativity drained the very life from the world. Finally, the world fell from its place high in the sky. Bruised and broken, it cried out in despair.

The world's cries of distress awoke the people all over the world. They all felt deep concern, seeing their beautiful world sobbing on the ground.

problems, would have a far greater chance of reaching solutions without inflicting injury - and even death - upon individuals. And we would be far closer to realizing the Global Vision.

Chaim Herzog, Israel

Science and technology may provide powerful tools, and scientists may take care to inform the public about their expected benefits and dangers, but it is society as a whole that must take responsibility for using them. Decisions about how to employ the fruits of science and technology will ultimately depend on what we value. Value judgments are made on the basis of moral and ethical considerations, and are often strongly influenced by social and political factors.

Ephraim Katzir, Israel

Although historians have not yet revealed the origin of people's active participation in society, it most certainly dates back to the dawn of mankind's history. Participation in society is imperative for the achievement, at least, of survival. Man throughout time has learned that his well-being is served best through association with others. Hence, contribution by participation is probably the most important feature in human civilization.

In recent times, people participation in the society has been stressed by all concerned with meeting the basic needs of human beings, let alone their development. National, regional and international organizations and agencies have fostered multi-purposed efforts to deepen and activate people's sustainable contribution in the community as well as in society.

Yet, in spite of all our efforts to enhance this sustainable contribution, the accomplishments attained were far from meeting human beings' needs and certainly far from fulfilling our aspirations.

There are many signs of people making effort to improve their society but more action needs to be taken to progress towards real development and satisfaction. The results achieved so far, even when measured by mere statistics, are not always encouraging.

Great technological advances have been achieved, particularly during the twentieth century, which have significantly improved the standard of living of the average person in terms of health, education and communication. However, as a result, a tendency has grown towards the pursuit of material gain, at the expense of a sense of positive participation amongst people in their society.

One of the related problems which I have noted during my involvement in voluntary work over the years, is the lack of enthusiasm amongst some people to participate and make solid contributions towards the betterment of their society, as a result perhaps of the pressure put upon them to ensure their own personal security. This inevitably leads to a certain degree of negativity and cynicism towards the upholding of moral and cultural values. Divisions have been created not only within communities, but also within the family home. Thus, the enhancement of community participation is essential, in order to prevent worry and fear from prevailing and to lessen human tragedy.

What are the real causes for the negative features noted in people's contribution? And on whom does the responsibility lie?

I refer the reader here to the heart of our Mt. Abu Declaration which states:

"We believe that any transformation of the world begins with the transformation of the self. For eventually, it is love, goodwill and cooperation which will overcome the negative forces threatening us and bring about the dawn of a new age."

It is really the self to which we should aim to direct our efforts to rebuild. It is in a society that can inspire and foster individual drives that humans can prosper.

Therefore, in order to fulfil individual responsibility towards ourselves, we should also accept responsibility for our community and society.

Local and national interests have broadened to encompass transnational concerns, and individual responsibility has equally been enlarged to incorporate relations and responsibilities beyond self and society.

In community participation, we should aim to encourage and support farmers who are tending their fields and improving their productivity, artisans who endeavour to perfect their jobs, teachers who are training and upbringing the new better generations and parents who endeavour to raise a self-assured child. Such aspirations can make life more worth living.

Everyone needs to work and earn a living in order to survive, but it is freedom, love, dignity, and self-respect which give people the initiative and creativity to raise their standard of living, to develop rather than to survive, and to inspire and be inspired towards attaining a better society.

Our only hope for salvation lies in preserving, or perhaps, returning to the moral and spiritual values that furnish us with freedom and love, and direct our path to hard work and fruitful cooperation, without which positive participation cannot be achieved.

We need to remember that active participation cannot be based on power, but on love and self-respect. Therefore, we do need, at the global level, a new psychological and mental formula which respects the special features, philosophies, and cultures of human beings on this globe, and understands and appreciates the common positive spiritual values which prevail in, and are needed for, a better world.

As St. Mathew wrote, many years ago: "Blessed are the meek, for they shall inherit the Earth."

It is common spiritual values such as this which will build and sustain the better world that we seek.

H.R.H. Princess Basma Bint Talal, Jordan

At first they all started to accuse each other, but eventually they realized it was no one's fault. They all sat back feeling helpless. No matter how hard each one tried to do something, it wasn't enough. Soon they began to wonder: could the world ever get better?

Then suddenly one stood up. "I've got an idea! Instead of trying one at a time, let's all try together! By cooperating with each other surely we can make the world better!"

The world, as I see it, clearly and distinctly, away from the shadows and scars of cold brutalities and stifling prejudices, is a world, a home, accommodating the diversities in religion, culture and creed with warmth, peace, compassion, cooperation and love. Each day has its own challenges in a multi-religious, multi-racial and multi-cultural country like Malaysia. This challenge of maintaining an equilibrium in religio-socio stability, concurrently with economic progress, helps to focus my vision, observe each day afresh and act decisively towards a just, equitable and an innovative administration. Watching this nation, a member of the world family, rise above mundane trivialities and differences, and advance with unity and harmony, strengthens my belief and hope that peace and prosperity will certainly prevail in the whole world. As is the vision of the people for a better world so will be the transformation of the world.

Prime Minister Mahathir bin Mohamad, Malaysia

What we need is a revolution in present day values and concepts, a revolution in changing fierce competition into collaboration for the common good rather than only for our own good. One has to look differently at all sorts of competitions in life in a different way than we do. Open competition without higher motive generates dislike and divisiveness, sometimes hatred; the objectives of competitions at school, at sports and later in life, must and certainly can be turned into a mutual companionship to achieve perfection and excellence in what one undertakes. If we are ready to reduce our selfishness, our greed for power or material things, then we can look at our neighbour as a friend who needs our help rather than as a potential competitor.

President Censu Tabone, Malta

The world will indeed be better if: the good which is inherent in every human being prevails over any negative and destructive attitude; the love which is limited to one's own kith and kin is extended to all human beings at home and abroad; the notion of self yields to a notion of service to the whole of mankind; the greed for power and domination yields to a yearning for equality of all men and women irrespective of creed and colour; dialogue and compromise replace confrontation, haughtiness, autocracy and bigotry in all spheres; it becomes a world where East and West do meet and are one.

Prime Minister Sir Anerood Jugnauth, Mauritius

Man is the only being on earth who can use his capabilities to engage nature and other human beings in order to continuously improve his station in life. This interaction with nature and other human beings can lead to the infringement of the rights of others and the encroachment of their territory. However, as beings with reason we should respect the rights of our fellow beings as well as protect our environment. While practising our own cultures we must be imbued with understanding and tolerance for the beliefs, values and norms of others.

Now that the Cold War has ended organizations such as yours are charged with the duty to bring us all together in an atmosphere of peace, respect and understanding. Technology and science have made our planet small and interdependent; at the personal and societal levels we must show the same sense of crossing barriers.

President Sam Nujoma, Namibia

The doctor stepped forward and gave concern. The mother stepped forward and gave tolerance and love. The businessman stepped forward and arranged funding.

World peace is the thirst of all human beings around the world. So let us all cooperate with clear hearts and minds to create "A BETTER WORLD" where there is love, unity, peace and harmony among each other.

The Rt. Hon. Nagendra Prasad Rijal, RPM, Nepal

My own vision for a better world is one where we accept and enjoy the differences between peoples with tolerance and understanding respecting all creeds and races for their unique contribution to the world.

Governor-General Dame Catherine Tizard, New Zealand

Like politics, international affairs is the art of the possible. No matter how clear one's vision, one cannot realize it alone. A small country like New Zealand is well aware of that. We are internationalists. We have to be committed to full participation in the cooperative, multilateral process. So if our vision is to take into account the ideal of international cooperation, what does New Zealand want, as a partner in the future of planet earth? I can tell you, simply, that my country and I share a "vision" and a "system" with 182 other countries. We share the ideals of the United Nations Organization.

Just as there is no sanctuary on earth from nuclear radiation, environmental problems, like climate change or ozone depletion or marine pollution, know no boundaries. A coordinated international response is required to address the problems. And of course the United Nations comes into its own in coordinating such a response. It will also prove to be a test of the commitment of member nations to our common future. It will take vision. It will take hard work. As the Mt. Abu Declaration makes plain, our world is a barren one without those qualities. We do have a common future. And we have a common forum. We must harness one to the other if we are ever to change the world.

Russell Marshall, New Zealand

If there is to be democracy, there must be unrestricted freedom of expression and thought. The media should help to educate people and further their development. Radio, television, weekly publications

The child gave her innocence, the politician lent his support. The old couple, the teacher, the accountant, one by one all stepped forward and helped in whatever way they could.

and newspapers should be ways of helping consolidate peace and democracy. In Nicaragua the basic function of the media should be to help to achieve national reconciliation, because this is the foundation our people needs in order to work in a patriotic and civic-minded spirit to achieve moral, political and economic reconstruction. As President of Nicaragua, I will resolutely encourage the establishment of communications media, because I am convinced that if there is freedom of the press there will be democracy.

President Violeta B. de Chamorro, Nicaragua

In our century, the pace of global change has never ceased to accelerate. The scale of human activity is now growing so rapidly that it is seriously undermining vital support systems for life on our planet. Yet we continue our behaviour in the present and our planning for the future as if events will follow previous patterns of experience. What we need today is a global vision of what kind of world society we want to leave to our children and grandchildren, and a concrete strategy of how we can make this vision a reality.

My global vision is one of a sustainable world society in which we have eradicated world poverty and restored respect and harmony with our global environment. It must be based on democratic rule, on respect for fundamental human rights, on social justice, on nondiscrimination and equality between races and sexes, and on the rule of law. It is a society in which the basic human needs of all world citizens are guaranteed. This global vision is not a Utopia. We can create it ourselves, if we act now. Several of the processes now threatening the global environment will become irreversible if we allow them to continue. Our generation may be the last to have the option of choosing this future. A failure to respond now means closing the options for those coming after us.

The World Commission on Environment and Development called for sustainable development as the only viable strategy for global change. We must take care of the needs of the present through a dedicated effort to erase world poverty and to reverse ecological degradation. But we must also make it possible for future generations to meet their needs. Instead of rapidly withdrawing assets from the natural resource base left to us by our ancestors, we must start investing in the kind of future we want to leave to our children.

A stronger, more effective international organization is not an end in itself. But it is becoming a vital and urgent necessity in our work to create a sustainable world society. The nation state is no longer an adequate institution for taking responsible policy decisions on transboundary matters which concern our common future. Some national authority must be surrendered through an international pooling of responsibilities, through institutions with supranational powers in matters which are vital for the survival of life on earth.

We must create a more humane world society, in which solidarity with our fellow human beings becomes more important than the accumulation of wealth. Such a society cannot come about by market forces alone; it requires active, wilful political management both at the national and international levels.

My global vision is of a social democracy, based on freedom, democracy and the full participation of all layers of our societies in our work for environment and development. If we manage to mobilize the tremendous human and technological resources which exist in the world society today, I am convinced that we will succeed in saving our common future.

Prime Minister Gro Harlem Brundtland, Norway

The priest and the yogi worked together and united the people of all religions to give the world back its soul, its life. At last the world was again filled with truth, peace, hope and harmony.

I am convinced that truth should be an inseparable ingredient of a new better world. I am a Christian. I believe that this religion contains fundamental values that all the people of the world should agree upon regardless of which faith they belong to. Besides truth, other fundamental values are justice, hope, love and the ability to forgive wrongdoings. Such ethics which are valid in interpersonal relations should be transferred onto an international level. The fundamental question which will decide the future of the world is whether or not political leaders of the superpowers will be able to work out an ethical style of political activities in relation to smaller and economically weaker states. Without new political ethics we will not be able to create a new world.

President Lech Walesa, Poland

The movement to the civilization of the 21st century won't be either simple or easy. It is impossible in a day to get rid of the heavy inheritance of the past or of the threats arisen in the post-war years. We experience a turning point in international affairs, and are only at the beginning of a new, I hope, mainly peaceful, long-standing period in the history of civilization.

I am an optimist, and I believe that jointly we shall be able to make a right and worldwide historic choice, not to lose a great chance at the crossroads of centuries and millennia, to pass the present ever-hard transition to the world order. Not a balance of powers, but a balance of interests; not a search for profit at the expense of others, but a search for compromises and consensus; not a claim on the leadership, but a respect for an equality - these are quite easy conditions for the sensible people grown wise with the experience of the twentieth century, people who can serve as a foundation for such a worldwide movement forward.

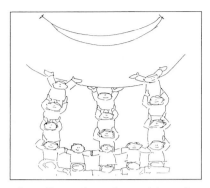

Then all joined together and formed a ladder to the sky. One by one they passed the world up and returned it to its proper place in the sky. Together they did what none of them could have done on their own.

The future prospect of a real peaceful worldwide policy lies in the creation of one international democratic space where the rights of man, welfare for citizens and assistance in asserting the same rights and such welfare everywhere, will be a priority of the state. This is an imperative for the growing integrity of the modern world and interdependency of its parts.

Mikhail S. Gorbachev, Russia

This type of initiative has a special usefulness, not only for the goodness of the objectives which are put forward, but also as a means of bringing to society's awareness the serious problems implanted in our world and the values which will help to solve them, as it is only with the endeavours of all that it will be possible to build a society of well-being for the enjoyment of all people.

Prime Minister Felipe Gonzalez, Spain

In the current phase of international transformation what we need is patience and perseverance in pursuit of a new world order where love and respect for the individual will prevail. We are all for a world where people enjoy intensively their individual rights and liberties and where democracy functions in a more profound manner than has ever been.

Aware as we are of the challenges lying ahead, tolerance and solidarity are the two basic features required of us if we want to lay the foundations of freedom, peace, progress and prosperity in the world. Dialogue is and should be the key to solve all disputes. Cooperation should replace hostility. People should at last come to grips that they all have a common interest in each other's well being and prosperity. These considerations led me to launch the "Black Sea Economic Cooperation Project" for the Black Sea Countries and to propose a "water peace pipeline" for the Middle East.

We in Turkey, encircled in an area of turbulence, are maybe the most willing of all to contribute to a peaceful transformation in the world and hope that our region gives the first signal that the world has matured enough to digest a new world order.

Turgut Özal, Turkey

Here in Uganda, for a number of years we have seen and experienced internal conflicts either between religious groups or tribal and ethnic groups, and sometimes, conflicts caused by political mismanagement of our society. All those conflicts have caused suffering of the people, destruction of property and slowing down of the economic and social development of the people.

We read in mass media, we listen to radios and learn also from friends from all over the world that almost every part of the world has been experiencing conflicts which result in violence. It seems either the world has never been at peace or that the human race has not learned how to live in peace. It may also be that we all do not understand what peace is all about and we seem to ask the question, "Peace for what?"

It is also true that internal conflicts always tend to spill over the boundaries of every nation and therefore involve as many countries as one can imagine as if we must always be at war with each other, both at home and all over the world.

Everyday I count incidences of misery, poverty, ignorance, backwardness, etc, etc, and I wonder whether or not, as an individual, I have the capacity to deal with so many problems our people in Uganda experience. Like everybody else, at the end of the day, I have to go home hoping tomorrow will be a better world for Uganda, but all seems to be day and night dreaming. However, through cooperation with so many other persons of goodwill both at home and in the larger world those problems we all face can be solved.

Vice-President Samson B. M. Kisekka, Republic of Uganda

Once again, the world was strong, healthy and happy - just as it was in the beginning - high in the sky where the sun shone on it all the time.

The purpose of raising children within the family is to provide the full range of support to enable them to take advantage of their own skills and qualities and to develop their potential to the utmost. Of course, individuals are responsible for their own actions. But everyone has a better chance of developing their talents with the support of their family behind them. Of course within the family, as a microcosm of society, the strong have a duty to support and encourage the weak. There are individuals within society who provide support outside their family for individuals and groups. We should applaud those who take this view and make this contribution to support their fellow humans.

Prime Minister John Major, UK

We have a vision of a new partnership of nations that transcends the Cold War. A partnership based on consultation, cooperation, and collective action, especially through international and regional organizations. A partnership united by principle and the rule of law and supported by an equitable sharing of both cost and commitment. A partnership whose goals are to increase democracy, increase prosperity, increase the peace, and reduce arms.

I see a world of open borders, open trade and most importantly, open minds; a world that celebrates the common heritage that belongs to all the world's people, taking pride, not just in hometown or homeland, but in humanity itself. People everywhere want much the same things: The chance to live a life of purpose; the chance to choose a life in which they and their children can learn, and grow healthily, worship freely, and prosper through the work of their hands and their hearts and their minds.

We are not talking about the power of nations, but the power of individuals. The power to choose, the power to risk, the power to succeed.

George Bush, United States of America

People from all around the globe had become closer and understood each other better.

AND...

THAT IS HOW GLOBAL COOPERATION FOR A BETTER WORLD BEGAN!

Visuals: George Edwards, Australia
Text: Stephanie Chin, Australia

There are many challenges that face our world today. Despite their number or magnitude, there are none that we cannot meet successfully if we wisely tap our tremendous natural and human resources in efforts of global cooperation. Each of us has an obligation to make the world a better place for future generations. We can begin by joining together throughout the world in mutual respect and concern to confront the challenges before us.

Jimmy Carter, United States of America

My dream of a better world is where everyone is free from want. Where all the components of modern living are accessible to all. My dream for a better world is where the earth's resources are shared by all its inhabitants. Indeed, there's plenty of everything to go around. The haves should show the have-nots how to produce enough.

Abdul Aziz Abdul Ghani, Yemen

CHAPTER SEVEN

INTERNATIONAL REFLECTIONS

Reverence for all life.

The preamble to the United Nations Charter begins with the words "We the Peoples". Since its creation in 1945, the membership of the United Nations has grown from 51 to 183 Member States representing the vast majority of the world's population. Although the world has changed dramatically over the past 47 years, the basic hopes and aspirations of people around the world today remain consistent with the vision of the future shared by the Organization's original founders.

The United Nations was created out of a commitment to "save succeeding generations from the scourge of war,...to reaffirm faith in fundamental human rights,...to establish conditions under which justice and respect for...international law can be maintained, and to promote social progress and better standards of life in larger freedom..." These goals were not envisioned by a government or institution - they were the product of human commitment and creativity directed towards the creation of a better world. Similarly, the attainment of those objectives requires continuing and concerted effort not only by governments, international and regional institutions, but by dedicated individuals throughout the world. In the second half of this century we have witnessed unprecedented technological developments - the exploration of outer space, the invention of the artificial heart, global communications by satellite. At the same time, the map of the world has been transformed with the independence of over 100 new sovereign states. The recent end of the Cold War and the current transition of Eastern European states to new democratic systems of government highlight the continuing possibility of dynamic political change. These and other developments are the result of visions shared by inviduals, who took practical steps towards their realization.

Progress is also accompanied by new challenges. The spread of nuclear weapons technology, the threat of environmental degradation, humanitarian emergencies, and the global debt crisis continue to challenge human creativity and commitment in finding solutions. There are no easy answers.

As we look to the 21st century, we should take pride and derive assurance from our accomplishments. The progress of the past provides the foundation for our future. Based on the commitment to create a better world which is so clearly shared by people in every region, I have every confidence that new challenges can be met and that international cooperation will assume ever greater importance in our continuing efforts for the future.

H.E. Javier Perez De Cuellar
Chairman, Commission on Culture and Development

Respect for the dignity and integrity of every human being.

In a better world, a balance would have been reached between the Earth's people and the national resources that sustain them. Rapid population growth would no longer exacerbate poverty and impede socioeconomic progress in developing countries. Priority would be given to qualitative improvements in the social sector, health care, education, and other aspects of human development.

Opportunities would be provided for each individual fully to develop his or her capabilities. Women would be given the opportunity to participate in and contribute to their respective societies on an equal basis with men. And in a better world, men would have it no other way.

A clean, fresh and balanced environment.

The Figures

In 1950 world population was 2.5 billion. Today we live in a world of 5.4 billion people; another billion will be added by 2001. Ninety-five per cent of this growth will be in the developing countries. The fastest growth is often in the poorest countries.

The Consequences

Poverty and rapid population growth combine in a growing threat to the environment and development.

What Do We Need?

* *An end to poverty* - a future for the "bottom billion" poorest people.

* *Clean technology* - development without damaging the environment.

* *Human-centred development* - better health, education and social services, including family planning for all who want it.

* *Status of women* - investment in women is the key to development.

* *Slower population growth* - to help meet development goals.

The Future

Sustaining our earth depends upon achieving a balance between population, resources, the environment and development. Reducing overall population growth will help. Urgent action is needed now: responsibility for the future begins today.

Nafis Sadik, Executive Director, UN Population Fund

Healthy and content in spirit, mind and body.

Shelter, food and water for all.

You, as young people have the chance to participate in something extremely important which has never been done before - something which will not merely earn a page in history, but will change history entirely, and for the better. It is an opportunity which did not even exist until very recently, and frankly, no generation yet has been able to achieve it.

When nearly 40,000 children die every day for largely avoidable reasons, then it becomes not only tragic, but unconscionable. In any civilization, morality must march with capacity. Today this means that the mass deaths of children must be placed alongside slavery, racism and apartheid on the shelf reserved for those things which are simply no longer acceptable to humankind.

Reducing child death rates worldwide by <u>half</u> in such a short period of time has never, in the past, been reasonably possible. Today we know it can be done. But it can be done <u>if</u> - and only if - people the world over take a dynamically active role and <u>make</u> it happen.

I urge you to seize the challenge and make this unique possibility a reality - for all the children - and the future - of the world.

James P. Grant, Executive Director, UNICEF

The attainment by all peoples of the "highest possible level of health" is my vision of a better world. The preamble to WHO's Constitution defines health as "a state of complete physical, mental and social well-being and not merely the absence of disease or infirmity". WHO considers health through equity and social justice to be a fundamental human right. The full exercise of this right is dependent on, and essential to, peace and security on this planet Earth. Health is an inseparable part of socioeconomic development.

Our task is to build for a better world. We must strive not only to comfort the sick, relieve pain, treat diseases and save human lives but also to ensure that the long life now potentially attainable will have meaning and quality. To achieve this, we need health care systems that, in my view, must be characterized by three major factors: (1) continuing improvement of the efficiency and effectiveness of technical interventions; (2) compatibility with the socio-political system and integration in national economic development; and (3) respect for human rights, such as the right to be informed and the integrity of the individual, including the freedom to take decisions in a spirit of social justice and equity. This is my vision of the future, and this is what we must strive for, with all the will, imagination, and energy we possess.

Hiroshi Nakajima, Director-General, World Health Organization

Individuals at peace with themselves.

The future of mankind depends on us, on each of us, each in our own way. It is our shared and individual responsibility, yours and mine. Indeed, it is only with the assistance of everyone, the support of everyone, each of us working in our own way in accordance with our means and potential that such a huge task can be accomplished. Peace is neither an unattainable ideal nor an abstract concept. It is very tangible: it is above all a right, the legitimate right of every individual to be able to develop, free from the threat of destruction, in harmony and justice, with self-respect and respect for others.

It is the right to security without inequality, to respect for such fundamental values as human rights; it is the right to live free of threats, the right to satisfy one's hunger, to work, to live in decent conditions, and above all to live in dignity. All that is peace.

In order to attain this goal, there must be first of all an awareness, and then a sense of responsibility. Everyone must understand that not only do they have a role to play, but that their role, whatever it may be, however small it might appear can, a priori, be a decisive factor for the future of mankind.

No society can truly benefit from the elimination of poverty, from development and from a better standard of living, unless people are able to enjoy their fundamental rights and freedoms. A society which thinks only in terms of material goods will never be able to escape poverty. Quite the contrary, a healthy society is one that sees development as a spiritual, cultural and material balance. Countless events throughout history have taught us this simple truth, but so far we have not been able to benefit from it.

My vision of a better world is one in which poverty would no longer exist, where threats, violence, destruction, crime and the undermining of personal integrity would be eliminated once and for all; it is a world of peace, in which everyone would participate in the development and progress of mankind with confidence, in harmony, dignity and solidarity. It will be a difficult task, one that seems almost impossible. But despite the immense obstacles, with the assistance of everyone, with goodwill and especially with the triumph of the fundamental principles of justice, tolerance and solidarity, we should be able to succeed.

Ambassador Jan Martenson, Sweden

Social, economic and political justice, as well as respect for human rights.

Love, trust, friendship and understanding in all human relationships.

A loving and fulfilling life.

In the months and years ahead, international cooperation to protect our planet, build sustainable development and begin the long healing process of our living environment will move from an ideal to everyday priority. In the face of the growing ecological crisis people everywhere are united in their resolve to prevent environmental destruction, and build bridges of confidence joining north and south, east and west in a common goal. We stand on the edge of a new world order, a new global imperative comprised of equitable, sustainable development. Our atmosphere, oceans, soils and fresh water, the biological riches of our forests and marine life constitute a common heritage we borrow from future generations. The decisions we make every minute of the day shape our children's future. My personal vision is therefore one in which inter generational responsibility unites us all in peaceful and equitable world order.

Mostafa K. Tolba, United Nations Environment Programme

My vision is of a world in which the economic needs and aspirations of its people can be brought into harmony with the earth's environment and resources through a transition to sustainable development. It is a world in which human beings can enjoy dignified lives free from absolute poverty, and in which people have come to terms with their relations among themselves and with the earth.

Maurice F. Strong, Secretary-General, UNCED

Transnational corporations have become an important source of global economic change, through the worldwide spread of foreign direct investment, their dissemination of technology and skills, and their role in integrating nations and regions into the world economy. The numerous benefits these corporations bring, however, tends to obscure their many activities that slip between the cracks of regimes of national governance and international convention. In some cases, pricing practices and movements of foreign exchange by trans-national corporations can frustrate national fiscal and macro-economic objectives; in other examples, foreign production can be accompanied by increases in toxic wastes, global warming and the incidence of industrial accidents.

In an era of heightened democratic aspirations, international measures of governance will increasingly be called upon to fill some of these gaps and move the activities of transnational corporations away from the law of the jungle of the international marketplace and towards a system of laws and regulations that can foster economic growth and equity.

Peter Hansen, Executive Director, Commission on Global Governance

Equal opportunities and encouragement to develop individual potential.

Poverty, in particular, is as much a scourge as war, and as great a threat to human security. Yet our planet has the capacity to sustain a human habitation in which everyone is peaceful in spirit, happy in mind and healthy in body. What we need is the acknowledgment that our humanity is inseparable, the will to put an end to otherness, and the resolve to live by neighbourhood values in our one world.

Sir Shridath Ramphal, Co-chair, Commission on Global Governance

Freedom of expression, movement and action, while respecting the rights of others.

We all seek a world in which knowledge improves human lives. Science and technology are the fruits of knowledge, but it takes compassion and judgment to put science and technology to work for human development. This means using science to help the people learn and to prevent disease, and using technology to eliminate poverty and still preserve our common environment. This requires good teachers, active grass roots organizations, a creative business community and most of all, an enlightened national leadership. We have choices in all countries, rich and poor, and we must make the right choices now.

William H. Draper III, Administrator, United Nations Development Programme

Economic growth as a kind of "Religion" has to come to an end with developed countries, allowing the third world countries to improve their living standard without causing too much harm to the global environment. To combat the threat of the forthcoming climatic catastrophe requires global efforts and sacrifices by the strongest and not the poorest.

Willy Straub, Secretary-General, Confederation of European Agriculture

A better world is where stewardship of the earth and its living and physical resources is practised by all, rich and poor; reliance is on renewable materials and processes to supply food and energy needs; and population growth is brought under control so that all can enjoy the earth's finite resources.

Mohamed T. El-Ashry, Chairman, Global Environment Facility

Frank communication at all levels of society.

The responsiblity of being a global citizen can be accepted on many levels: however the most important and effective level of action is often within local communities. This concept is especially important for youth to understand since they are the next leaders of the global community. Thus, today's youth must be empowered through education to maintain a global perspective while making a difference in their own neighbourhoods.

Zohreh Tabatabai, Co-ordinator, Fiftieth Anniversary, United Nations

Visuals: Manolo Galdon, Spain

CHAPTER EIGHT

WE THE PEOPLES FOR A BETTER WORLD

Sculptures by Lydia Sperlich in her roof garden in New Delhi, India. (Kris, UK)

I have come to realize that America's fundamental truths "that all people are created equal, that they are endowed by their Creator with certain inalienable Rights, that among these are Life, Liberty and the pursuit of Happiness" were meant for all people in all parts of the world. Unfortunately, we the American people have not yet been able to apply these truths even to our fellow countrymen. In our brief 200 year history, America has gone from the golden land of freedom and independence, to a land of isolation, violence and corruption. This nation of "we the people" was founded on the principle of "in God we trust" yet spiritual identity and spiritual values seem to be a missing piece for many Americans. My hope lies in an understanding that a transformation within this country is underway. Many citizens are making the choice not to accept the level of isolation that has become so prevalent. Instead they are reaching out to reconnect with God and their fellow-man. These architects of change are starting to work together at the local, national and international levels in an effort to inspire others to become involved in the re-creation of a better world. Many now understand that "we the people" are the people of the world not just of one nation. We have been blessed with the freedom of choice and it is now time for each of us to take personal responsibility for helping to create a better world.

Rita Cleary, Corporate Consultant, USA

What is the role of politics in the transformation of the individual and society? I asked myself this question in 1987 when I won a seat in the Senate of the Philippines. After a number of years in national politics, I now realize the enormous potential of politics and government in changing society for the better.

Political reform with an ethical dimension essentially takes place at three levels - individual, national and global. From the individual to the global seems to be an unreachable goal, but that can be achieved if the combination of politics and ethics is used for that purpose. The change, however, must begin with the self - this is basic. Without the internal transformation of the individual, there is no possible external change. On the other hand, an intimate knowledge of political realities must orient the internal person. In the field of politics, that individual who is to symbolize change should be the political leader himself or herself, supported by followers imbued with the same need for individual and societal transformation.

But the self must not be imprisoned within the shell of the ego; it must go beyond such narrow confines and discover its own essence in God whose nature is joy, peace, love, as well as power and justice.

This personal link with the Infinite, or a principle beyond the self, must not be broken even in the field of politics. With a leader willing to transcend the self, he/she can serve and transform others. A dark room gradually becomes bright when a single candle lights up a hundred others. In this way, a social movement is created and the cleansing and restructuring of society is made possible. Think of the achievements of Mahatma Gandhi or Nelson Mandela. Their lives prove that *right is might*. But the counterforce to that is: might is right - as asserted by Josef Stalin and Adolf Hitler, who brought violence, untold suffering and death in their wake.

This brings us to the important point that values are both means and ends. If political and moral transformation is the goal, the means to achieve that goal must be imbued with an ethical and social conscience. Let us remember that genuine political movements for change did not merely depend on financial power or the use of physical force. Rather, it was the inner strength of people, their sheer commitment and cooperation for a common cause which brought down dictatorships in the Philippines and in Eastern Europe. The fervent desire for change made the Berlin Wall crumble and is finally breaking the barriers of apartheid in South Africa. In spite of years of oppression and abuse, people continue to struggle for certain values in their daily lives and for their country such as respect for human rights, the elimination of graft and corruption and the establishment of democratic institutions.

But there are other values which are also necessary for global change. For countries of the developing world, values like self-reliance, national dignity and evolving an authentic culture in an interdependent world are important for their survival. For the developed countries, a renewal of traditional values as well as respect for the rights of weaker nations. But whatever the level of economic growth, countries must maintain in their very societies values such as respect for individual dignity, accountability in public office, and discipline in community life. The values required at the global and macro levels may seem too abstract and distant for the average man and woman but the values are essentially the same both for the private and public spheres: truthfulness, honesty, and the transcendence of the spiritual side of life.

Although major political changes have occurred world-wide, recent experience has shown, however, that after the first chapter of political change, the vision can fade, the inspiration dries up and before we know it, there is a return to the *status quo ante*. Thus the history of many nations the world over is a series of aborted and truncated movements for national and global transformation.

How can movements be best institutionalized? How can the original vision, in the beginning so bright and clear, be translated and sustained into an organized but dynamic bureaucracy?

The United Nations has played an enormous role in helping to promote peace and define the requirements of economic development. It has assisted developing countries to prosper more systematically and

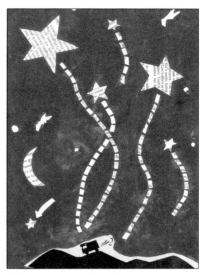

"The Journey to Stars",
Panom Sethakorn, Thailand

has helped to shift the power systems of the world, although slowly and sometimes imperceptibly. Yet, for all of the advances in planning techniques and scientific knowledge, so much poverty and despair, both material and spiritual, remain in developing and developed countries. In our daily lives, we witness the signs of a world bereft of ethical awareness - the daily eruptions of violence, breakdown of the law, disease, graft and corruption. For this reason, the *what* and *how* of life must be continuously recreated.

It is time to renew the vision, to strengthen the global network, organize and manage bureaucracies and administrations which will respond to politics with a social and moral conscience. In 1987, I launched in the Philippines the Moral Recovery Programme with the sub-theme: "Building a Nation, Inspiring our People to Action". I wanted to bring back the power of ethics into the arena of politics. This was in response to what I saw as a hunger for moral and spiritual renewal in our political and collective life.

Our experience in the Moral Recovery Programme which continues to grow, despite limited resources, points out the following: 1) there must be an analysis and reflection by the people themselves on the moral and ethical crisis of their nation; 2) there must be strategies for value transformation in relation to the objectives of the various components of government and the private sector (for instance, the police and postal authorities require value orientation); 3) there must be a basic structured approach in small groups for learning and monitoring value transformation.

In many countries of the world, movements for politics with an ethical and social conscience have emerged. Will peoples of the earth and their leaders seize this opportunity to create a better world? Let us hope so. Our collective and political lives must be transformed by God's power and purpose.

Leticia Ramos Shahani, Senator, Philippines

"The Choice is Yours", Mary Lou B Roldan, Marc Ajon, James Sotto and Maribeth, Philippines

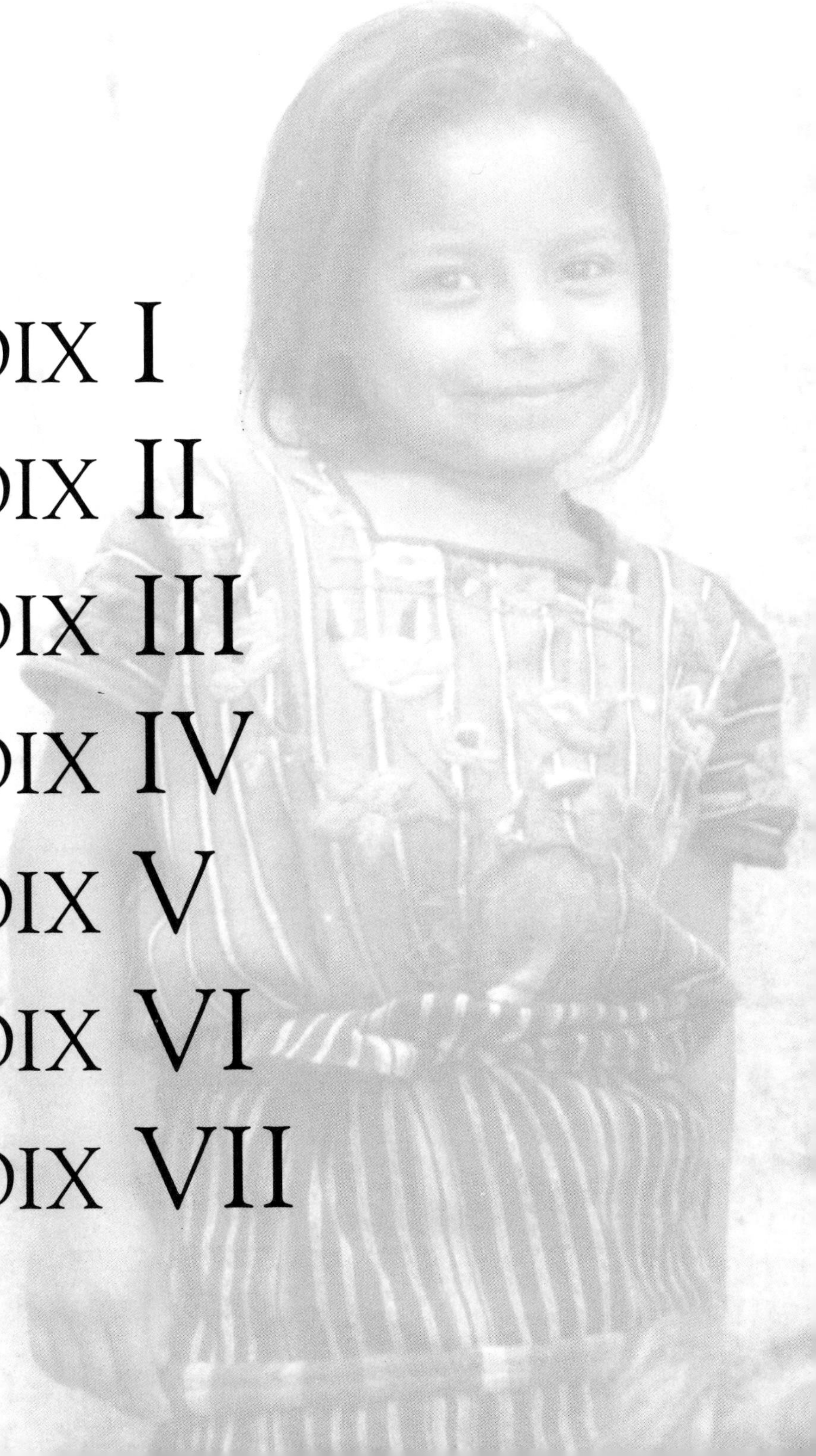

APPENDIX I
APPENDIX II
APPENDIX III
APPENDIX IV
APPENDIX V
APPENDIX VI
APPENDIX VII

APPENDIX I

WHAT IS YOUR VISION OF A BETTER WORLD?

Yesterday's vision is today's reality and today's vision will be the reality of tomorrow.

Shuby Dewan, Professor, USA

WRITE <u>YOUR</u> VISION BELOW.

DON'T FORGET TO USE THE GOLDEN RULE!

At the heart of Global Cooperation is a GOLDEN RULE: Draw upon the pure core of goodwill that lies at the centre of the human spirit and create a vision of the world in purely positive terms rather than allowing doubts, concerns or fears to colour the future. Think positively!

_____

_____

_____

_____

_____

_____

_____

_____

_____

_____

_____

_____

_____

_____

_____

_____

APPENDIX II

ON RUNNING CREATIVE GROUPS AND ROUNDTABLES

The Creative Group Workshop methodology used world-wide by the Global Cooperation project can be useful to help get people involved in defining and initiating positive change.

The workshop is ideally suited for about 10 people, requires about two hours and has the following objectives:

1.   To create a shared vision of a better world.
2.   To define the essential methods and values within the vision.
3.   To decide on recommended plans of action to implement the vision.

Procedure:

1.   *Explain the Golden Rule:*
      Draw upon the pure core of goodwill that lies at the centre of the human spirit in order to create a vision of the world in purely positive terms rather than allowing doubts, concerns or fears to colour the future. Think positively!

2.   *Moment of Silent Reflection:*
      Invite the members of the group to sit quietly for a few minutes to create an image of a better world in their minds. Ask the group the following questions:
      -What kind of a better world do I want?
      -What kind of relationships do I want within that world?
      -What do I want to be like - what kind of characteristics would I like to have?

3.   *Sharing and Building the Vision:*
(a)   Ask each one to share his or her image of a better world.
(b)   After discussion and agreement on the main aspects, summarize the vision by writing up the suggestions on a big sheet of paper.
(c)   Ask the group to choose which aspect they want to discuss in-depth i.e. Self, Relationships or Surroundings. Remind the group of the Golden Rule.
(d)   Allow time for each one to share his or her vision of whichever aspect the group has chosen. Encourage positive alternatives to negative suggestions. Summarize the vision and identify the values within the vision. If time allows, discuss the other areas in greater depth too.

4.   *Action Planning:*
      Review the vision in silent reflection for a minute. Invite the group members to decide what action they want to take to help make their vision of a better world a reality and whether to do so together or individually.

5.   *Rounding Off:*
      The group members discuss what they feel they have learned or gained by being part of a creative group and share their experiences of working together.
      Decide whether to have another session either to continue to create the vision, formulate an action plan or carry it out. Decide on the topic, date, time and venue.

Creativity, Communication and Cooperation

Human Resource Development Consultant Rebecca Ortega of the Philippines, who helped develop the Creative Group format for Global Cooperation, shares below some of her experiences of the universal appeal and effectiveness of Global Cooperation group discussions.

The Golden Rule, which encourages the use of positive ideas and language and the extensive use of visualization, proved to be very effective in Creative Group meetings or workshops in breaking the ice between opposing group members, stopping the bickering and starting a meaningful dialogue. As you might expect in any group of people, some came with their own personal agendas, or fixed beliefs, or felt that they were personally carrying the burden of trying to solve the world's problems as well as their own. The primary focus of each Creative Group was to enable each participant to interact as a person in his or her own right and only secondarily on the basis of any professional expertise or position. I found that there were three main components in a successful group session - creativity, communication and cooperation.

Creativity: The use of the Golden Rule in creating a mental picture of the desired future world encouraged participants to go beyond their usual way of thinking. They were also encouraged to express themselves in an artistic form in order to enhance teamwork and cooperation and they often presented their vision and action in dance, song, sketch or mural. These group presentations turned out to be the highlight of the workshop. They provided opportunities to share and discover hidden talents and artistic skills. This affirmed individual self worth and enhanced mutual respect and appreciation.

Communication: The use of positive ideas and positive language eliminates barriers to communication. People tend to pay attention and listen more to positive and creative ideas. The more people listen to and understand each other's ideas and opinions the more they are affirmed as persons. True communication is enhanced in a non-threatening and supportive atmosphere where individual contributions and ideas are acknowledged unconditionally by the group members. Mutual acceptance leads to trust and confidence in each other. The best indication that there is smooth communication is the lightness and happiness generated during the interaction process.

Cooperation: A main ingredient in a cooperative endeavour is the aspect of identifying the common goals or tasks of those involved. This is provided by the consensus building approach within the Creative Group Process. Visualization of the desired future greatly helped in identifying and clarifying commonalities of vision and ideas. The use of positive language to express ideas and vision encouraged a clear statement of the common vision. The Creative

Project coordinator Rebecca Ortega leads a workshop with mothers of malnourished children in a nutrition centre in Metro Manila, Philippines.

Group approach enhanced mutual respect and acceptance among the members. One good thing in any cooperative task is that leadership is shared and everyone is focused on the group goal or task rather than on a leader. The Creative Group approach provides a shortcut in the formation of working groups. This is possible simply because the approach prevents the occurrence of conflict among the group members. Instead it provides for open, supportive and trusting communication. It also ensures the easy and quick unfreezing of participants due to the built-in positive, non-threatening atmosphere encouraged by the Golden Rule. Positivity makes it easy for people to deal with their own feelings and reactions towards each other. Conflict, argument or even minor disagreement drains the creative or productive energy of the group. The positivity of the approach provides opportunities for developing and enhancing relationships among members rather than mending or making up broken relationships which is characteristic of problem-solving or decision-making groups. Hence relationships tend to be lasting and more permanent. Positive qualities such as tolerance, flexibility, understanding and respect are developed and practised during the session.

Rebecca Ortega, Human Resource Consultant, Philippines

A Simple but Significant story

This is a very simple story, yet very significant because in a very special way it changed my life. I think that everything that relates to life is significant. I am a 63 year old woman and at that time of your life you do not think much more will come your way than has already been offered to you.

Most of my life I have been alone and having lost both of my parents at the age of 14 I learned to be independent, locked up inside and not expecting anything from anyone. So much so that when a conflict arose between me and my closest friend and neighbour in a small town just outside Warsaw I said to myself: "Well that is just fine". Fifteen years passed by and my friend and I did not exchange one word.

Last year I had to go to Warsaw for a while. One evening in a small community centre I found myself sitting amongst a group of people who were talking about a vision of a better world - a vision of the future. I was reluctant - I drew back and listened - careful as always, not letting myself open up, not trusting and careful not to get involved. But I watched and as I watched I began to smile against my own will. The people were strangers to me, some young, some older and yet what they were saying was not strange to me. They were sharing their hopes, their dreams, their expectations of a better life, a better world and as I listened I felt myself being drawn in. Suddenly I realized that I also wanted to share - share what I think, what I desire, what I would like to see in the world, people, life and myself.

I saw how these people, although strangers to each other, shared the same hopes, dreams and wishes. As the evening progressed I found myself in an atmosphere of such warmth, as if all barriers had been broken. For the first time I realized that other people were not my enemies, they were human beings just like me with true and beautiful feelings deep inside them. I felt as if a knot suddenly had been untied releasing all the real feelings of trust, willingness to reach out to others, communicate and cooperate, feelings of acceptance and understanding.

All that had been opened up and was free flowing. I watched with my eyes wide open and my heart melting and changing. Then there was the closing of the session and I was asked what I would do now in my life, something practical to bring that vision of a better world closer to reality. I thought for a moment and I said: "Well, I have a friend with whom I have not spoken for 15 years - I must go and see her."

Maria, retired, Poland

Vision of Creative Group, Switzerland. Marie Binder, France

GLOBAL COOPERATION ROUNDTABLES

Global Cooperation's Roundtable Groups are similar in format to that of the Creative Groups but usually continue for at least three to four hours and typically include a dozen or more professionals who then break into smaller groups to focus on one or two topics in detail. The Roundtable format provides an opportunity for a dynamic and cooperative dialogue building towards an agreed vision of selected areas of life in a better world.

In essence the procedure is to:

1.   Decide upon several key topics such as health, education, family, business or community.
2.   Create a vision of a better community, family life, education system and so on.
3.   Define the essential values or principles underlying the vision.
4.   Decide on action plans to help make the vision a reality.
5.   Discuss and define principles of cooperation i.e. factors that can facilitate cooperation.

Roundtable on the River Volga, Russia, hosted by the Soviet Peace Commitee. (Kishore Solanki, UK)

In our group (at the Science Symposium in Greece) there were scientists from eleven countries, from both developing and industrial nations. It was a beautiful experience of just being able to meet as human beings, as individuals who had a concern about the interaction of science and the environment. There was a lot of give and take. I am hesitant to use the word cooperation. Cooperation is a process. The work here involved a kind of initiation because we were put together. I think if we were to meet again there would be real cooperation and the achievement of consensus. It takes time to establish a rapport.

What I did see happen, though, was an accommodation of others' scientific views and a gradual appreciation of their respective world views. I think accommodation first and foremost has to come before cooperation. The minute you open your mouth, other people have to accommodate what you are saying and be very patient with you and try to follow through your thought process.

What I encountered during the entire week was deep compassion for other people, nations, professions and predicaments.

Wanjiku Mwagiru, Ecologist, Kenya

APPENDIX III

THE GLOBAL VISION SEMINAR

Even amidst the often extreme adversity of life in the world today signs of hope can often be seen. They seem to brighten in step with growing recognition of the ability of the individual to take charge of his or her life. For this we must take stock of shared hopes and wishes, assess inner convictions and then adopt appropriate values and action plans. As a contribution to this process the Australian Advisory Committee of Global Cooperation developed and piloted "The Global Vision Seminar". The format and methodology are described in a facilitator's manual and video from which the following extract has been taken.

THE CONTENT:

Your vision for yourself and the world will stand on the foundation of your values. The direction you take in life is a result of the values you choose. At every step you are making value judgements according to the priority you have placed on certain values.

Identifying values is empowering. It clarifies what you stand for. It gives you commitment to following those highest values and gives you the basis on which to choose the right course of action at the right time.

Sharing values is uplifting. As people in groups, organizations, societies and in the world share values, they realize that the core values which bind us together are so much greater than the things that set us apart.

THE OBJECTIVES:

(a)   to identify the core values which underlie The Global Vision Statement;
(b)   to identify the barriers which prevent us from adopting and living those core values;
(c)   to develop strategic action plans (organizational, community or personal) in order to overcome those barriers and thus make The Global Vision Statement a reality.

THE AGENDA:

Introductory Plenary:
> Welcome; explanation of Global Cooperation; presentation of The Global Vision Statement; identify core values underlying the Statement; divide into twelve small groups, one for each point of the Statement.

Values Workshop:
> Exploration of what values are from a personal perspective; discuss what values underlie the group's allocated point of the Statement and can enable it to become a reality; agree on the three main underlying values.

Values Plenary:
> Presentation by each group of its three selected values; identify three core values that underlie the whole Global Vision Statement; identify barriers in bringing these values into action at personal, organizational and community levels; divide into four small groups.

Barriers Workshops:
> Reflect on what obstacles prevent implementation of the identified values; agree on three key obstacles; identify the problems, contradictions or value-clashes that cause obstacles to arise or lead to paralysis in implementation of plans.

Barriers Plenary:
> Presentation by each group; agree on three major barriers; divide back into same four groups.

Strategies Workshops:
> Discuss and develop strategic action plans that will help overcome the identified barriers and allow the chosen values to be expressed more fully in personal, organizational and community life; agree on the six strongest plans.

Final Plenary:
> Presentation by each group of its six agreed strategic action plans; as a whole group, reflect on all core values, barriers and plans.

Feedback:
> Evaluate the day's proceedings and make a personal commitment to carry out chosen strategic action plans; closing remarks.

APPENDIX IV

COOPERATION IN THE CLASSROOM

Global Cooperation's project pack for teachers, "Cooperation in the Classroom", provides a programme of practical activities to promote children's appreciation and practice of cooperation.

Specially prepared by three English teachers - Anthea Church, Lesley Edwards and Eugene Romain - the pack was piloted in the UK (by the Nottinghamshire Education Authority) and the USA (by the New York City Board of Education). 40,000 copies have already been distributed free of charge world-wide among 30 countries in Arabic, English, Chinese, French, Hebrew, Russian and Spanish and the pack has been approved by at least 11 national and many local educational authorities.

The pack contains a bank of activities for students to work on together which will provide them with focused practice in the skills of cooperation. These opportunities for practical experience are accompanied by a section on using the activities as part of an ongoing programme for children's social skills development. The pack is an expression of optimism about the way children can work together, if they are taught how, and the real pleasure teachers can get if they are willing to dedicate energy and patience to helping them.

Cover of Global Cooperation School's Pack, "Cooperation in the Classroom". (Martin Lord, UK)

The pack is divided into different sections outlined below:

1. Setting the context

"Cooperation - A Complex Art"

	Intellectual Skills e.g. Imagine Question Concentrate Decide Anticipate	
Physical Skills e.g. Talk Listen Watch Co-ordinate Write	Interpersonal Skills e.g. Encourage Explain Understand Reciprocate Help	Personal Qualities e.g. Humour Openness Discretion Enthusiasm Sincerity
	Attitudes to Others e.g. Respect Appreciation Patience Positivity Support	

Cooperation is a complex art requiring us to function on several levels at once. It requires physical skills, intellectual skills and interpersonal skills. In addition, it involves certain attitudes to those people with whom we are cooperating. And combining all these skills and attitudes in the manner appropriate to any situation calls for a wide range of personal qualities.

Children's ability to cooperate will improve quickly if they receive the following: activities which stimulate development in each of the five areas below; activities which provide an opportunity to practise the flexible combination of these five areas; and frequent language practice to develop the accompanying vocabulary and deepen awareness and appreciation.

2. Teacher's Notes

"Getting the most from working together"

The students of New York are faced with the greatest challenge of all, for due to the fact that New York is such a multicultural conglomerate, their vision will truly reflect conflicts germane to almost all ethnic groups.

It is from this perspective that I welcomed the project, and gave warm support to its educational pack, *Cooperation in the Classroom*, for use in our public schools. This wonderful programme engages children in cooperative activities which develop critical thinking, interpersonal relationships, positive attitudes and an understanding of and appreciation for the diverse cultures represented in their school. The activities stress team work and the ability of youngsters to work together harmoniously as they exert their creative talents in envisioning a better world.

I am indeed happy to state that *Cooperation in the Classroom* has been introduced and implemented with great success in an ever-increasing number of community school districts in New York City. This well researched and carefully designed educational bank of activities will have a positive effect on the children and will undoubtedly make a world of difference in their concepts and attitudes about life, other people and the world in general.

Pearl M. Warner, Former Executive Director,
Curriculum & Instruction, New York City Board of Education, USA

3. Activities for working together

"Making things together - White Towers"

Students are divided into groups and, after making a design, must build a tower as strong and attractive as possible within a limited time, with limited materials, and in silence. Creativity and communication are essential in agreeing upon the design and cooperation in implementing the design without talking.

New York school teachers in the middle of tower building (Raj Bhagirathee, USA)

St. Bernadette Primary School children speaking about their model of an ideal village, Lagos, Nigeria. (F.O. Olayinka, Nigeria)

4.   Working with the world in mind

Working together to produce the model village was marvellous for all participants. It gave us happiness and joy to serve our fellow men in creating a better world. We have also shared the joy of working together and contributing our individual views and support. It also gave us the hope that every group endeavour brings success. It has implanted in us the burning desire to cooperate in our own ways to create a better world. We believe that a better world can be created out of the small world of each individual. Through the model village we could catch a glimpse of the world of harmonious existence of human beings and animals.

Children and staff of St. Bernadette Nursery & Primary School, Nigeria (submitted by F.O. Olayinka, Nigeria)

5.   Activities for the photopack

The pack includes 16 photographs which can be the basis of a variety of activities such as describing the scene or asking who, what, where, when, how.

"Hope", a photo for one of the activities in Global Classroom School's pack, Cooperation in the Classroom. (John Urich-Sass, Mexico)

APPENDIX V

UNITED NATIONS PEACE MESSENGERS

*A*lthough the United Nations is unique in its broad international membership and mandate, the organization does not work alone in its efforts to create a better world. The United Nations carries out its tasks as part of a dynamic network of governments, intergovernmental organizations, non-governmental organizations, grass-roots groups and individuals. Each of these contributes, in its own way, to the creation of a more secure and peaceful world. The activities of non-governmental organizations (NGOs) are an important component of this continuing global effort.

The United Nations works closely with NGOs, research institutions and cities worldwide in order to encourage and coordinate efforts for the promotion of peace and annually observes the International Day of Peace. In this context, there is now a broad network of NGOs and cities designated as "Peace Messengers". This special designation is given by the Secretary-General in recognition of their contributions to peace and in appreciation for their continuing cooperation with the United Nations. Following the International Year of Peace (1986) the United Nations Peace Studies Unit was formed to encourage organizations and cities to work together with the United Nations for the promotion of peace and to coordinate Peace Messenger activities.

In a world of rapid and often unexpected change, recognition that people share many common values can provide an important source of stability and solidarity. Such values also provide important perspectives for future action. Despite differences of nationality, culture or philosophy, people around the world share many common values. The desire for a just and peaceful world, a clean environment and equal opportunities for health care and education for all people are among the visions of a better world which are shared by people from every continent. "Global Cooperation for a Better World" has provided important insight into the values which so many people share - and their potential for taking effective action toward their realization.

The Global Cooperation project, sponsored by the Brahma Kumaris World Spiritual University, contributes important impetus to local and grass-roots efforts toward a more secure and peaceful world. The project began in 1988 and was the first project to be designated as a "Peace Messenger Initiative Dedicated to the United Nations". In over 120 countries, the project has encouraged people to translate their thoughts about a better world into appropriate action in homes, schools, and communities. The work of such individuals and organizations is an essential complement to the efforts of national governments and the United Nations. The creation of a better world is clearly a task for everyone.

Dr. Robin A. Ludwig,
United Nations Headquarters, New York

APPENDIX VI
PARTICIPATING COUNTRIES
COUNTRIES FROM WHICH VISIONS WERE RECEIVED

Algeria
Argentina
Australia
Austria
Bahrain
Bangladesh
Barbados
Belgium
Bhutan
Bolivia
Botswana
Brazil
Burundi
Brunei Darussalam
Bulgaria
Cameroon
Canada
Chile
China
Colombia
Commonwealth of Dominica
Costa Rica
Cote D'Ivoire
Croatia
Cuba
Cyprus
Czech Republic
Democratic People's Republic of Korea
Denmark
Ecuador
Egypt
El Salvador
Ethiopia
Fiji
Finland
France
Germany
Ghana
Greece
Guatemala
Guyana

Haiti
Hong Kong
Hungary
Iceland
India
Indonesia
Iran
Iraq
Ireland
Israel
Italy
Jamaica
Japan
Jordan
Kenya
Kiribati
Kuwait
Latvia
Liberia
Libyan Arab Jamahiriya
Madagascar
Malaysia
Mali
Malta
Mauritania
Mauritius
Mexico
Micronesia
Mongolia
Morocco
Mozambique
Namibia
Nepal
Netherlands
New Zealand
Nicaragua
Nigeria
Norway
Pakistan
Papua New Guinea
Paraguay

Peru
Philippines
Poland
Portugal
Puerto Rico
Republic of Korea
Romania
Russia
Rwanda
Saudi Arabia
Senegal
Sierra Leone
Singapore
Slovakia
Solomon Islands
South Africa
Spain
Sri Lanka
Sudan
Suriname
Swaziland
Sweden
Switzerland
Syrian Arab Republic

Taiwan
Thailand
Togo
Tonga
Trinidad & Tobago
Tunisia
Turkey
Uganda
United Arab Emirates
United Kingdom of Great Britain
& Northern Ireland
United Republic of Tanzania
United States of America
Uruguay
Uzbekistan
Vanuatu
Venezuela
Viet Nam
Western Samoa
Yemen
Yugoslavia
Zaire
Zambia
Zimbabwe

APPENDIX VII

A NOTE ON THE EDITORS

Brahma Baba, founder of the Brahma Kumaris.

The work of the Brahma Kumaris World Spiritual University is inspired by the vision of a world where every individual can develop to his or her own full potential as a human and spiritual being, and live in harmony with others and with the natural world. Founded in India in 1936 by Prajapita Brahma, the University is now an international organization with over 3,700 branches in sixty countries, and works at all levels of society seeking to help bring about positive change in the world. It offers a range of educational programmes in moral and spiritual values aimed at building a greater awareness of the worth and dignity of the human person.

The curriculum is based on the recognition of the intrinsic goodness and spirituality of every human being. Education in spiritual principles is combined with the development of latent qualities and the strengthening of personal power.

In a world of declining standards, disintegrating values and rapid unpredictable change, the University seeks to heal by offering a spiritual understanding of the self and the world. It teaches a practical method of meditation which helps individuals to achieve peace of mind, develop their full personal potential and interact with others in a constructive and fulfilling way. This brings an increasing awareness of the value and potential of life, a deeper sense of self-identity, clearer judgement, greater self-respect and a more stable personality. These are the springboards for greater mastery of the self, right action and harmonious relationships.

The courses, classes and lectures aim to balance the rational and intuitive faculties of the intellect, and provide each individual with the ability to call on his or her inner resources and strengths in any situation. Teachers and students from the University also visit community centres and organizations, prisons, hospitals, schools and businesses to conduct seminars, workshops and dialogues on the development of personal skills, meditation and better ways of working and living together.

The Brahma Kumaris World Spiritual University has coordinated and participated in numerous UN activities. Its contributions have been recognized by the UN, from which it has received seven UN Peace Messenger Awards. Its activities support UN programmes on human rights, the environment, development, youth, women, health, drug and substance abuse, child welfare, disarmament and other humanitarian issues. In 1980, the University became affiliated to the United Nations Department of Public Information as a non-governmental organization. It has had consultative status with the UN Economic and Social Council since 1983 and with UNICEF since 1988. The Brahma Kumaris World Spiritual University was the principal coordinator of "The Million Minutes of Peace" during the UN International Year of Peace in 1986. In April 1988, to continue the work of the Million Minutes, the University launched "Global Cooperation for a Better World", the first Peace Messenger Initiative dedicated to the UN.

Each Brahma Kumaris centre and its activities are funded and run by teachers and students who live and work in the local community. Courses and classes are mainly held in the early mornings and evenings. All activities are offered free of charge as a community service and, although the University is registered as a charity in many countries, it does not raise funds and all its teachers are volunteers. While the University is administered by women, participants in its activities come from all backgrounds and ages and no pre-qualification for attendance is required.

The University's activities outside India are coordinated from Global Cooperation House, its International Centre in London, with the assistance of a world-wide network of regional offices. The World Headquarters is located in Mount Abu, Rajasthan, India and is the main decision-making body of the University.

SHARE VISIONS WITH A FRIEND

VISIONS OF A BETTER WORLD - ORDER FORM

FORMAT: 8" X 10", 220 Pages with over 100 colour and 100 black and white illustrations

QTY

_____	SOFT COVER EDITION	(ISBN 0-9637396-8-9)	US$19.95/£12.99	_____
_____	HARD COVER EDITION	(ISBN 0-9637396-9-7)	US$24.95/£16.99	_____

SHIPPING & HANDLING (Inland only*)
15% of your order - min. US$ 4.00/£3.50   _____

*For Shipment overseas, and for larger orders, please enquire.
All prices are subject to change.   TOTAL _____

☐ Cheque/draft/money order enclosed
☐ Charge my credit card   (USA only)   ☐ Visa ☐ Access/Master Card
Card Number ☐☐☐☐☐☐☐☐☐☐☐☐☐☐   Expiry Date _____

ORDER FROM YOUR LOCAL BOOKSELLER OR DIRECTLY FROM:

Literature Department
Global Co-operation House
65 Pound Lane
London NW10 2HH, UK
Phone: 0181-459-1400
Fax: 0181-459-6793
(Payable to Brahma Kumaris Literature)

U.N. Bookstore
GA-32B
New York, NY 10017, USA
Phone: 1-800-553 3210
Fax: 1-212-963 4910
(Payable to UN Bookstore)

Global Harmony House
46 South Middle Neck Rd.
Great Neck, N.Y. 11021, USA
Phone: 1-516-773-0971
Fax: 1-516-773-0976
(Payable to Brahma Kumaris)

Allow 1-2 weeks for local delivery; 4-6 weeks for overseas delivery.
The book may also be obtained (price available on request) from other UN Bookstores and from the Brahma Kumaris at:

78, Alt Street
Ashfield, Sydney
NSW 2131
Australia
Phone: 61-2-716-7066
Fax: 61-2-716-7795

Global Co-operation Museum
P.O. Box 12349
Maua Close, off Parklands Road
Nairobi, Kenya
Phone: 254-2-743-572
Fax: 254-2-743-885

P.O. Box No. 2
Mount Abu
Rajasthan 307501
India

PLEASE PRINT

SHIP TO:

NAME:_____

ADDRESS:_____   SIGNATURE

_____   DATE

TELEPHONE NO: _____ FAX NO: _____

VISIONS OF A BETTER WORLD - ORDER FORM

FORMAT: 8" X 10", 220 Pages with over 100 colour and 100 black and white illustrations

QTY

____	SOFT COVER EDITION	(ISBN 0-9637396-8-9)	US$19.95/£12.99 _____
____	HARD COVER EDITION	(ISBN 0-9637396-9-7)	US$24.95/£16.99 _____

SHIPPING & HANDLING (Inland only*)
15% of your order - min. US$ 4.00/£3.50 _____

*For Shipment overseas, and for larger orders, please enquire.
All prices are subject to change.   TOTAL _____

☐ Cheque/draft/money order enclosed
☐ Charge my credit card   (USA only)   ☐ Visa ☐ Access/Master Card
Card Number ☐☐☐☐☐☐☐☐☐☐☐☐☐☐☐☐   Expiry Date _____

ORDER FROM YOUR LOCAL BOOKSELLER OR DIRECTLY FROM:

Literature Department
Global Co-operation House
65 Pound Lane
London NW10 2HH, UK
Phone: 0181-459-1400
Fax: 0181-459-6793
(Payable to Brahma Kumaris Literature)

U.N. Bookstore
GA-32B
New York, NY 10017, USA
Phone: 1-800-553 3210
Fax: 1-212-963 4910
(Payable to UN Bookstore)

Global Harmony House
46 South Middle Neck Rd.
Great Neck, N.Y. 11021, USA
Phone: 1-516-773-0971
Fax: 1-516-773-0976
(Payable to Brahma Kumaris)

Allow 1-2 weeks for local delivery; 4-6 weeks for overseas delivery.
The book may also be obtained (price available on request) from other UN Bookstores and from the Brahma Kumaris at:

78, Alt Street
Ashfield, Sydney
NSW 2131
Australia
Phone: 61-2-716-7066
Fax: 61-2-716-7795

Global Co-operation Museum
P.O. Box 12349
Maua Close, off Parklands Road
Nairobi, Kenya
Phone: 254-2-743-572
Fax: 254-2-743-885

P.O. Box No. 2
Mount Abu
Rajasthan 307501
India

PLEASE PRINT

SHIP TO:

NAME:_____

ADDRESS:_____

_____

SIGNATURE
_____

DATE

TELEPHONE NO: _____ FAX NO: _____